THE EXAMINED LIFE

THE EXAMINED LIFE

by

Daniel Rose

Copyright © 2019 by Half Moon Press.

All rights reserved. No part of this book may be reproduced or transmitted in any form or by any means, electronic or mechanical, including photocopying, recording, or by any information storage or retrieval system without written permission from the publisher. Write Half Moon Press, 480 Park Avenue, New York, NY 10022.

Published by Half Moon Press, New York, New York.

Printed in the United States by Cenveo Publisher Services, Philadelphia, PA

Library of Congress Control Number: 2019916713

ISBN: 978-0-578-58686-1

Cover painting by Herbert Katzman

Author photo by Karen Hunt-Kolczynski

TO MY CHILDREN

AND GRANDCHILDREN

WHO ARE THE JOY OF MY LIFE.

CONTENTS

Preface . . . . *i*

ESSAYS AND SPEECHES

Looking Ahead: Toward an American Narrative for Today . . 1

"The Worst There Is Except For All the Others" 5

Doing Good, Doing Better: The Role of
    Private Philanthropy 11

American Education in the 21st Century 19

Much Crime, Little Justice – Why? 23

America's Identity Crisis – "What Am I?" vs "Who Am I?" . . 25

Fresh Thinking on Social Class 29

Should Undergraduates Study History? 33

Heraclitus and 21st Century American Judaism 37

Evolving Cities – Demographically, Economically,
    Physically 43

THE HARLEM TIMES EDITORIALS

Your Child, The Genius 53

The Community Role in Education 55

Hi Tech and Black Employment 59

Ta-Nehisi Coates—Looking Backward or Forward? 63

On Heroes and Hero-Worship:
   Commemorating W. E B. DuBois 67

Amazon, Gentrification and Silicon Valley East 71

Future-Mindedness and Child-Raising Today 73

A Hero for Today 77

PERSONAL VIGNETTES

Dr. Martin Luther King, Jr.
   and the March on Washington 83

HEAF and Black Education 85

The Queen of Western Samoa and the Cub Scouts 87

Housing For the Performing Arts 89

Boston's Thriving Waterfront 93

Pat Moynihan and Federal Healthcare 97

Barack Obama and Hamlet's Mother 99

The Tribal Chief and the Goat............................101
Pentagon City: The Urban Village 103
Lincoln Center..105
Times Square 109
Adolf Eichmann in Jerusalem..........................111
Debating the Mullahs 113
Horace Mann and Tilly 115
American Exceptionalism at its Best..................117
East Hampton—A Fifty Year Love Affair...............121
'Chicken Little' and Economic Forecasting. 125

ADDENDA

Jewish Week 131
Marquis Who's Who 137

PREFACE

The pages that follow were written at a time when much of our society seemed worried about the present and anxious about the future, when our national leadership and our political and social institutions seemed unequal to the challenges they faced, and when angry polemic displaced the reasoned discussion we desperately need on crucial public issues.

Crying out for rational, evidence-based examination are such topics as education, criminal justice, social diversity, personal identity, even fundamental questions of how to grow the national economic pie and how to divide the proceeds more fairly. I have suggested some answers and hope they will stimulate others.

This volume represents essays, speeches and articles on many topics and also contains my articles from The Harlem Times and personal memories.

I hope you find the pages thought-provoking.

Daniel Rose

ESSAYS AND SPEECHES

LOOKING AHEAD –
TOWARD AN AMERICAN NARRATIVE
FOR TODAY

At my recent college reunion, I reminded my 1951 classmates of our good fortune in having lived in America's golden years. The half-century from the end of World War II to the economic debacle of 2008 gave substance to the concept of "American exceptionalism," which is being questioned today.

The world acknowledged then our prosperity and global power, our social harmony and thriving middle class. The dollar was seen as the world's currency, English as the world language, jazz and Hollywood movies as the world's entertainment. We were the economic engine of the world – inventing, designing, manufacturing for those around the globe. Almost any (white, male) American willing to work hard and follow the rules could find stable work and an acceptable lifestyle.

That world no longer exists. In some ways it is better today: racism, anti-feminism and homophobia are recognized as moral failings; our gross inequalities are a national embarrassment and our traditional belief in a level playing field for all children is seen today as a noble but unrealized aspiration. On the downside, socio-economic upheavals have shattered faith in leadership elites and in many of the political institutions whose effective functioning was fundamental to our sense of well-being.

High-tech innovation, competitive globalization, the changing of the nature of work – in an unstable and hostile multi-polar world – have caused anxiety about the present and foreboding about the future. Much of our public is frightened and feels victimized as incomes stagnate for many and dreams of upward mobility diminish. The public has lost confidence in the competence and integrity of our political leadership, in the fairness of our business administrators, in the truthfulness and reliability of our news media; and they question the ability of our social and political institutions to meet 21st century challenges.

We need a new national narrative and vision for the future, the American Dream updated for our times. We need an inspiring and optimistic vision of hope for social justice, for the greatest good for the greatest number, for the well-being of those who work hard and play by the rules.

The American Dream was never a guarantee of success but a guardian of opportunity, and we should strive today to provide all citizens with opportunities for personal growth and fulfillment. As our society opens more and more doors for those previously excluded, those formerly frozen out must be ready, able and willing to participate fully, benefiting from and contributing to the common good.

The new narrative must seek broad consensus and compromise between those focusing primarily on personal responsibility and those chiefly concerned about universal entitlements. We need understanding of the trade-offs between efficiency and equality, on what is due to the young vs. the old, the healthy vs. the impaired.

What we demand and what we can afford should balance, and our public must understand that the benefits and entitlements promised by political aspirants are feasible only in the context of a growing Gross National Product. No society can live indefinitely by borrowing from the future; and incentives necessary for increasing economic production put limits on expenditures. "Robbing Peter to pay Paul," may work in the short run, but for the longer term, Peter must have incentives and the motivation to keep producing.

An important step toward a renewed American Dream is the re-establishment of public trust in the competence and integrity of our national leadership. To be trusted they must be trustworthy; to be trustworthy they must accept the traditional "unwritten rules of the game" and the fundamental grounds on which democratic government rests: appropriate standards of probity and civility among our role models and character and ability in our leaders.

"Out of the crooked timber of humanity no straight thing was ever made," say philosophers. The inadequacies of our leaders, our institutions and of our voting public are facts of life. But high aspirations for a just and equitable society and a vision of how to achieve them are also part of the human condition. How to formulate, articulate, communicate and implement that vision is the challenge for us as citizens, despite our varying opinions.

We should use the best thought of our best thinkers, communicated by factually-supported presentations openly discussed by commentators representing a broad spectrum of viewpoints. What has been called "the vital center" should recapture public attention from the extreme right and extreme left that dominate public discourse today.

Education, healthcare and criminal justice; housing, recreational facilities, the creation and maintenance of physical infrastructure, the protection of historical landmarks; thoughtful consideration of the question of climate change – all merit rational and evidence-based discussion by our public leaders. We are entitled to no less and should demand no less. The challenges are clear, but the answers are elusive in an age the Oxford English Dictionary calls "post-truth," when ludicrous conspiracy theories and outright lies are disseminated by public figures.

Honorable, well-informed, public-spirited individuals must be heard, but even more importantly, they must be encouraged to enter public life. Politicians can become statesmen when properly supported, when their constituents value character and probity, and they respect patriotism (love of country) over nationalism (hatred of others). With good leadership, our society can again be motivated by "enlightened self-interest" (Adam Smith) or "self-interest properly understood" (Alexis de Tocqueville) that promotes the general good.

In ancient Rome, Marcus Aurelius noted that "what is not good for the beehive cannot be good for the bee." His disciples today understand that by improving public health, public education, public infrastructure and public safety, we are helping ourselves and our families, as well as "the beehive."

May 29, 2019

"THE WORST THERE IS, EXCEPT FOR ALL THE OTHERS"

Winston Churchill's famous comment on democracy as a political system applies as well to free enterprise capitalism as an economic system. No other economic form provides the incentives for economic innovation and creativity, relates the desires of the consumer to the efforts of the producer, encourages the voluntary savings and investment necessary for economic growth or effectively channels the skills, talents and energies of the public.

At its best, free enterprise capitalism provides unparalleled well-being; at its worst, it can be a dog-eat-dog, winner-take-all system that leads to turmoil and social upheaval. America's historic well-being and prosperity reflect the effective working of this economic form. Today, yellow lights are flashing and capitalism is under question and even attack.

In recent years, especially since the 2008 economic debacle, much of the American public has lost confidence in both the competence and fairness of our political leaders and our business establishment; they feel a loss of transparency and accountability. Increasingly they fear that our governmental institutions can no longer protect them in an age of high-tech innovation, globalization and the changing nature of work. As incomes stagnate or decline for many and dreams of upward mobility diminish, the huge new fortunes of the few at the top stimulate a loss of faith in American capitalism itself.

Astute business leaders increasingly point out to colleagues the need for reforms to preserve the system. Jamie Dimon of JPMorgan Chase, Ray Dalio of Bridgewater, Howard Schultz of Starbucks and Larry Fink of BlackRock are among those calling for higher taxes on the wealthy and a change of heart on the subject of short-term "shareholder value" as a company's goal. Jamie Dimon is explicit in declaring that acting responsibly toward a company's employees, customers and the community in which it operates is in the investors' longer-term interests.

Open public discussion and reasoned debate on these issues by our political leaders will help to educate a bewildered public to understand how free enterprise can work for them. Today more than half of Americans between the ages of 18 and 29 claim to prefer what they believe is socialism.

The confused (and confusing) comments about socialism by left-wing demagogues muddy the waters of economic discussion precisely when we desperately need clear thinking on the subject. Taxes on the rich and benefits for the poor are NOT socialism nor are government expenditures for the public good.

Socialism – a system by which the government owns the means of production and allocates the products – is what Castro's Cuba, Mao's China and Stalin's Russia imposed on their suffering people. Under socialism, central planning rather than consumer choice dictates production and distribution.

The Nordic countries today, admired by those on the left, are proud of the high productivity of their free market economies, with the proceeds prudently apportioned among their societies' varied stakeholders. They are NOT examples of socialism, but of enlightened 21st century capitalism at its best.

The challenge today for America's leaders—its political office holders, its business establishment and its public intellectuals—is to regain public trust and confidence by encouraging the free enterprise market to work better for the benefit of all.

Opinions will differ on what specific steps toward reform are indicated, but a thoughtful public will demand that our national leadership give reasoned, evidence-based consideration to nine fundamental problem areas:

A) No society can live beyond its means indefinitely. At some point (sooner rather than later) our national expenditures cannot continue to exceed our national income and our national indebtedness (which should be a subject of continuing public scrutiny and discussion) must reflect intergenerational fairness.

B) Future-mindedness, not obsession with short-term results, should dominate our thinking. The crucial factors for continuing long-term economic growth and well-being - the creation and encouragement of an educated and skilled labor force, the production and maintenance of appropriate physical infrastructure and continuing support for fruitful scientific research—must be acknowledged as pressing concerns. Research today determines production tomorrow.

C) Fair competition—not the "crony capitalism" of well-connected insiders—must be (and be seen to be) the aim of public policy. Government regulations that stimulate innovation and creativity will encourage the formation of new business. Public transparency is the best stimulant to fair and open competition.

D) Not "big government" or "small government", but "smart government" should be our goal, with a dollar's worth of value received for every public dollar spent. As a general rule, state expenditures tend to be more efficient than federal, and local more so than state.

E) Efficient, cost-effective healthcare (which is being achieved today by most other advanced nations) should become our carefully-considered, fairly-administered practice. Today we have higher per capita healthcare costs with less effective results than every European country.

F) A sustainable Social Security program, reflecting the increasing longevity of our population, must have appropriately re-considered charges and benefits. Adding two years to the age at which donors contribute and at which recipients benefit and raising the income level of donors subject to social security tax would strengthen the program dramatically, making it permanently self-sustaining (as it was originally planned to be).

G) Political campaign finance reform and re-examined lobbying practices would do much to restore public confidence and dissipate cynicism about "hidden government" and "shadow elites." With business contributions to political campaigns now in the billions, the concepts of "free speech" and "bribery" need examination and public discussion.

H) Thoughtful reform of our immigration policies and practices is long overdue. The terms and conditions relating to those we permit to cross our borders, and how we deal with those now here illegally deserve mature discussion and long-term consideration rather than frenetic polemic.

I) Tax reform is a must! The experience of all other advanced nations shows that taxes on consumption ("value-added" or sales taxes) are more efficient than taxes on income or wealth, which are easily evaded and sometimes counter-productive. V.A.T. will not be regressive if necessities (food, shelter, medicine) are exempted and if luxuries (furs, jewelry, yachts) are surtaxed. Some economies – Hong Kong and Singapore are examples – have modest taxes on financial transactions, which we may wish to consider, as an effective and relatively painless source of revenue.

Conclusion
Profit-seeking business in a competitive free-market economy, prudently regulated within a wisely-devised legal system overseen by

an honest and competent judiciary, is the most effective economic vehicle we know for providing a society with the wherewithal to finance the well-being of all.

Universal experience has shown that this is most likely to be achieved in a democratic society with effective scrutiny of the governing process, with a free press demanding answers to questions of legitimate concern and, above all, with public trust and confidence in the competence and integrity of the national leadership.

Committee for Economic Development
June 17, 2019

DOING GOOD, DOING BETTER: THE ROLE OF PRIVATE PHILANTHROPY

Today's economic climate has put governments under pressure to cut back on expenditures. Societies that traditionally depend on government for social and medical services, education and support for cultural activities as well as scientific research programs, must make difficult decisions. The prospect of private philanthropic help has become increasingly appealing and urgent.

All over Europe, purse strings are being tightened and cultural lights are being dimmed.

In the U.K., for example, many of Britain's 700 publicly funded regional museums are in jeopardy because of budget constraints. Five museums in Lancashire recently closed and five more in West Yorkshire are under imminent threat. The 30% cut in Department of Culture funding since 2010 has taken its toll, with attendance down over 10% at its fifteen sponsored institutions as entrance fees increase and services diminish. Forty-four local authority or trust-run museums have closed since 2010, with more to come.

The popular Northampton Museum had its accreditation removed by the Arts Council of England and was disbarred from the Museum Association after 'deaccessioning' its ancient Egyptian Sekhema statue for £15 million to cover operating expenses. This occurred just as the Art Institute of Chicago announced a $400 million gift from the Edlis family and New York's Metropolitan Museum of Art announced a $1 billion gift from cosmetics mogul Leonard

Lauder. Donations like these could occur in Europe, as they do at privately sponsored art museums like the Frick, Whitney, Guggenheim and Getty. Yale's Center for British Art (the collection of Paul Mellon) is the largest collection of British art outside the United Kingdom.

The Mausoleum of Augustus, Rome's first Emperor, is neglected, fenced off and closed to the public. Of Greece's 10,000 formally recognized archeological sites, fewer than 200 are open to the public. Yet Italy and Greece devote Europe's lowest share of public expenditure to culture. Somewhere there are private donors who could help, just as private donors support George Washington's home at Mt. Vernon or Thomas Jefferson's at Monticello and are funding extensive repairs to the Lincoln Memorial and the Washington Monument.

Private philanthropy in Europe has exploded in the last two or three decades, with Sweden in 2012 being the final European nation to introduce tax deductions for charitable giving. England was the first, introducing modest tax incentives in the 1920's, and some contributions followed. Today, every European nation encourages private philanthropy. Academic contributions from alumni are increasing and some European institutions, such as London's Imperial College and the INSEAD Business School outside Paris, are starting to attract multi-million dollar gifts.

The King Baudouin Foundation United States helps European non-profits to fund-raise in the United States; and the Tate Americas Foundation, founded in 1989, has raised over $300 million in support of London's Tate Gallery. American Friends of the Prado, American Friends of the Louvre, American Friends of the Israel Museum and similar groups look to American donors for support; but "home grown" private philanthropic funding is a largely untapped resource crying out to be harvested.

The wide range of European cultural influences and attitudes precludes a 'one-size-fits-all' charitable analysis. The historic role of the church or great families in founding or maintaining educational and health institutions has varied. Today, in general, where tax rates are higher, the proportion of private individuals who give is lower. Rates of charitable volunteering of time and effort vary greatly from country to country; and European public trust and respect for large philanthropic organizations range from high in the Nordic countries to low in Mediterranean nations.

How private philanthropy in Europe can be increased, and what lessons can be learned from American practice are questions that merit more attention than they generally receive.

The American philanthropic experience is unique, differing dramatically from that of all European nations. It stems from the tradition of a nation founded without a monarch, without a long-established landed aristocracy or a strong central church. If pioneers wanted a school, a hospital or a church, they had to build it. And they were grateful to fellow citizens who made it possible. Alexis de Tocqueville noted in 1835 that Americans believe that "self-interest rightly understood" involves association and cooperation for the common good.

Publicly-acknowledged and highly-praised private giving is embedded in the American psyche. Although many Europeans decry this practice and find it embarrassing, Americans cannot imagine large-scale philanthropy without it. When the Reverend John Harvard died in Cambridge, Massachusetts in 1638, leaving the local divinity school 800 pounds sterling and his library of 400 volumes, the school in gratitude renamed itself "Harvard College." When Elihu Yale donated goods sold for 560 pounds sterling to the Collegiate School of New Haven, the school was renamed "Yale College" in 1718. When Johns Hopkins of Maryland died in 1873 and left an unprecedented seven million dollars to found America's first research university and teaching hospital, there was no question about its name. Ezra Cornell, James B. Duke, Moses Brown, Leland Stanford, John D. Rockefeller and many others were proud to be identified with the institutions their benefactions made possible; and the public cheered and honored them. (Harvard's endowment is now $37 billion, Yale's is $26 billion and today 56 private American universities each has an endowment of over $1 billion. The Morrill Act of 1862 created America's public college system, but today even the public University of Texas has an endowment of over $25 billion.)

More recently, no one was surprised when little-known Oregon Health Services University announced that for Nike-founder Philip Knight's $500 million gift, it was creating the Knight Cancer Institute and the Knight Cardiovascular Institute. Stanford's new graduate fellowships (patterned after the Rhodes Scholarships) will also bear Knight's name, thanks to his recent $400 million gift. Cornell Medical College has just been re-named for Sandy Weill, after his $600 million gift.

On the other hand, Chuck Feeney (duty-free shops) has given away over $6 billion through his Atlantic Philanthropies, most of it anonymously; and world-famous M.I.T. was the creation of the anonymous "Mr. Smith" (Kodak's George Eastman). Whether anonymous or acknowledged, America's rich are encouraged to think of themselves as trustees of public wealth and those of great wealth who do not at some point give major support to some non-profit recipient are considered moral defectives.

To increase European philanthropic giving, tax laws should be simplified, and traditional cultural patterns of public praise for cotributors should be re-examined.

England bestows knighthoods on major philanthropists; France, the Legion of Honor; America awards Honorary Doctorates; but encouraging all citizens to feel proud of their contributions is an important step toward increasing those gifts.

American museums list the names of major donors on their walls, and major tax-exempt organizations publish Annual Reports listing the names and gift levels of donors, even the most modest. "Vulgar," "ostentatious," and "crude" are words often applied to U.S. fundraising techniques; but Americans, the most pragmatic people since the ancient Romans, reply, "Yes, but they work." If Europe wishes to replicate American philanthropic success, it should find ways to praise and encourage donors, while embarrassing the rich whose names are absent from the lists. (Italy, for example, could institute a "Lorenzo de Medici Award" for major philanthropic donors.)

Throughout America, philanthropic peer pressure from friends, neighbors, classmates and business associates is non-stop. Invitations to testimonial luncheons, dinner dances, theater parties, auctions and golf outings assault us. An avalanche of charity mail fills our mailboxes daily. And the numbers speak for themselves.

In 2016, the U.S. non-profit sector will reflect nearly $500 billion in fresh gifts, involving eleven percent of the total national labor force and constituting six percent of our Gross Domestic Product, having passed the national defense sector in 1993. In addition, charitable volunteers contribute the labor equivalent of more than five million full-time employees. Middle- and lower-income Americans give mainly to religion, the upper-income to education, culture and health; and foundations give largely to social service, scientific research and overseas programs.

The Ford Foundation, with its $12 billion endowment and its $500 million in annual grants, is world-famous for its international efforts at reducing poverty, promoting democratic values and stimulating achievements in the arts and sciences.

The Gates Foundation alone distributes more overseas aid than the entire Italian government; in its first two decades, the Gates Overseas Vaccine Program is estimated to have saved the lives of some eight million children. American churches and synagogues send four and one half times as much to foreigners as Gates does; and private American aid sent overseas exceeds the foreign aid budget of the U.S. government. ($39 billion to $31 billion respectively)

The most important point to be stressed in a discussion like this, however, is the widespread American conviction that in some areas of public concern — such as culture, education and scientific research — private philanthropy is more entrepreneurial, more cost-effective and more swiftly responsive to public needs than government. Innovation and creativity have usually begun with private philanthropy and then been implemented by government.

The Nobel Prizes won by scientists financed by Rockefeller University (resulting in penicillin, kidney dialysis, the yellow fever vaccine, etc), the 4,977 schools founded by Julius Rosenwald for black children (empowering a black middle class), the 2,509 public library buildings built by Andrew Carnegie (strengthening literacy nationally) — are all well-known and celebrated. In 2014, when the Ebola virus suddenly appeared in West Africa, high-tech billionaire Paul Allen pledged $100 million to fight it before governments seemed officially aware of the problem; and he pledged more millions to fight the Zika virus as soon as it appeared.

For health care, housing, education and social services, America's middle and upper income groups have been well-served by the free market for services for which they can afford to pay; but by European standards the U.S. poor are not properly served. John Kenneth Galbraith described this in his book "The Affluent Society" as "private affluence and public squalor." Clearly, American government has much to learn from the best European examples in dealing with the poor.

American foundations, too, are often criticized. The largest ones are attacked for extreme caution, excessive overhead cost and bureaucratic inertia. Some public foundations (for police, veterans and firefighters) give too little to beneficiaries and too much to fund-raisers. Some private foundations are seen as playthings for the rich, with exotic or trivial beneficiaries. Militants — liberal and conservative — periodically call for an end to tax exemptions, but the public feels that Bill Gates or Chuck Feeney can spend the revenue more cost-effectively than the government.

The challenge we all face is how to balance the roles of government, the free market and private philanthropy for the greatest public good.

America's chief governmental failures have been in efforts to educate the children of our poorest minorities; private groups are often more successful. In Washington, D.C. today, for example, only 48% of black males graduate from high school. In New York City, with lower standards, 65% of black students graduate from high school in four years, but school officials acknowledge that fewer than half of New York City students are classified as "ready to meet the academic demands of college."

As an example of what the philanthropic sector can accomplish in this area, I have been asked to describe the efforts of The Harlem Educational Activities Fund, a privately-financed, privately-supervised inner city after-school program my wife and I created twenty-five years ago.

Since then, over one thousand minority public or, as you call them, state school students have participated in the HEAF program, with 100% of the students graduating from secondary school and virtually 100% going on to four year colleges. While 11% of all U.S. high school students go on to graduate school, over 35% of HEAF students do. HEAF-sponsored inner-city minority chess teams have ranked Number One in U.S. national chess competitions, and the mentor of our chess team has, with HEAF financial support, become the first black U.S. International Grand Master of Chess.

What is the secret of HEAF's success? It does not preach "victimization," but inculcates future-mindedness and high aspirations, instilling the self-confident conviction that unremitting effort now will be rewarded with success in the future. 'Teaching' is what takes place in the classroom, 'learning' is what takes place in your head, HEAF proclaims, and HEAF's role is to help you to learn.

We tell our students, "your responsibility is to read, write, count, think critically and speak effectively on your feet. HEAF's role is to help you do so." "Time is the scarcest commodity in your life and you cannot dissipate it on video games and social media." "Always think ahead — failing to prepare is preparing to fail."

With such encouragement and emotional support, HEAF graduates become doctors, lawyers, engineers. One of our earliest graduates, from a dysfunctional inner city home, is today a Major in the U.S. Army who has just entered the Army's Command and General Staff College, on her way (we hope) to becoming a black, female General! She and her colleagues serve as role models for present and future generations, part of what W.E.B. DuBois, America's greatest black thinker, called "The Talented Tenth" who are the salvation of society.

The role of HEAF — and similar first-rate, privately-sponsored efforts like K.I.P.P. ("Knowledge is Power"), Harlem Children's Zone and the Success Academies — is not only to help individuals but also to demonstrate what can be achieved and to stimulate public endeavors. Private groups like "I Have A Dream," "A Better Chance" and "Prep For Prep" provide aid for promising children overlooked by government.

Do I believe in the role of private philanthropy? I do — and as in the case of Europe today — if it didn't exist, we would have to create it.

The 141 billionaires (largely American) who have signed the Bill Gates/Warren Buffett Giving Pledge of at least one half their fortunes to philanthropy deserve special thanks and recognition. And all who can afford to do so should follow their charitable intent, answering the biblical question "Am I my brother's keeper?" with the reply, "Yes, I am!"

Private philanthropy can provide donors with a sense of satisfaction and fulfillment while benefiting the common good in important ways, and it should be seen as a "win, win" game for all.

Thank you

Oxford Literary Festival
Christ Church College
April 8th, 2016

AMERICAN EDUCATION IN THE 21ST CENTURY

"I have not yet begun to fight!" shouted Captain John Paul Jones, before a fierce Revolutionary War naval battle. That could become the American public's reaction to the poor ratings our students receive in international academic competitions. Pragmatic Americans will, in due course, understand that changes in our educational attitudes and practices are overdue if we are to achieve the universal literacy and develop the skilled public we desire. Greater public attention and concern, greater allocation of public resources and greater respect for the educational process are all clearly demanded of us.

Other leading nations today understand that educated human capital is a more important national asset than financial, industrial or physical capital. Only the United States regards education as a private consumer good ("It is for your benefit so you pay for it.") rather than a public resource worthy of governmental investment for all appropriately qualified students from all backgrounds at all educational levels. Our current undervaluing of universal educational opportunities is reflected in our low national levels of upward socio-economic mobility and in the disparity in achievement between advantaged and disadvantaged demographic subgroups.

While our well-endowed best private universities and technical institutes are the envy of the world, no other advanced nation has such glaring imbalances in educational opportunities for its advantaged rich versus opportunities for inner-city minority poor or isolated rural young. No other advanced nation makes so little provision for vocational training or employment preparation for those unable to go on to higher education.

In virtually every other advanced nation, secondary school students are offered the choice between academic paths or vocational training tracks in which they spend years in paid apprenticeships in on-the-job learning experience. In Switzerland and Germany, for example, two-thirds of young people elect the occupational route, choosing employer-paid preparation for careers as skilled technicians—air traffic controllers, police officers, lab technicians, medical assistants and over 200 other specialties. At age of, say, 22, they have marketable skills, serious work experience and cash in savings accounts, instead of the typical American experience of suffocating student loans and uncertain employment prospects. At any time, apprentices can choose to switch back to an academic path if they wish.

Factors unique to the U.S. make educational reform difficult. Fifty individually-programmed state governments and 14,000 school districts financed by local property taxes present problems which are exacerbated by a polarized federal government.

Our non-profit colleges and scientific institutes are admired, while many of our for-profit colleges are seen as disgraceful scams victimizing a poor and unsophisticated clientele. Our elementary and secondary schools, varying widely in quality, are considered both among the world's finest and among the world's worst. Our nation's 1,300 community colleges, largely ignored by the well-educated middle class, are under-financed and under-utilized vehicles with great potential for giving functional training to the poor, the formerly incarcerated and non-English-speaking immigrants.

For public education to receive the support it must have to obtain the necessary resources, public intellectuals and educators must make a persuasive case for it. Fortunately, the factual basis for such a case is clear.

Decades ago the U.S. public understood that education does not "cost" but "pays." Economists pointed out that our government's best investment ever was the 1803 Louisiana Purchase from France and the second best was the 1867 purchase of Alaska. The third best investment, they said, was the post-World War II G.I. Bill, where lifetime taxes paid by college-educated veterans were much greater than those paid by their uneducated identical twin brothers. That additional tax revenue represented a great financial return on the scholarship funds advanced. Education still pays today, at all levels. Nobel Prize winner James Heckman has famously documented the great economic return on effective pre-school education.

Thoughtful observers have pointed out five educational problem areas that merit immediate attention and open-minded discussion:

The level playing field we need for all our pre-school children, especially for their "first 1,000 days," which are crucial to the child's attitudes, self-confidence, motivation and socialization;

Higher standards for the selection, training, remuneration, retention and promotion of primary and secondary school teachers (along with greater respect and higher pay for teachers as skilled professionals);

The total re-thinking and re-planning of our under-financed and under-utilized community colleges;

College-level provision of STEM and professional training (along with exposure to general education) for all properly qualified students;

Encouragement and support at federal and state levels and by private philanthropy of scientific research, upon which future innovation, development and national well-being depend.

Fair-minded observers will take different positions on these topics, but our national well-being requires informed discussion and appropriate action by our national leaders and thinkers.

Every nation's pool of aptitudes and talents is reflected in a bell-shaped curve of human possibilities. Those societies best able to provide opportunities for every child to realize its full potential (whether through higher education or other training) will flourish. When a student's high potential is unrealized, we all lose.

America needs a national conversation on how to meet this challenge and how to devote the appropriate resources to education. From 2008 to 2017, state funding for public two-year and four-year colleges declined by $9 billion and average tuition in public colleges increased by 28%. Average student loan debt for 2017 graduates was $28,700, yet 60% of all Americans support tuition-free public colleges. We have a lot to talk about.

Counselors of Real Estate
March 27, 2019

MUCH CRIME, LITTLE JUSTICE—WHY?

The United States has 5% of the world's population but nearly 25% of the world's prisoners, including juveniles. After serving their jail time, two-thirds of our former prisoners are back behind bars within three years, three quarters within five years of release. (Norway's five-year recidivism rate is 20%, Germany's is 33%, Canada's is 35%.) An estimated 160,000 imprisoned Americans are serving life sentences versus 59 in Australia, 41 in England, 37 in the Netherlands. The severity of our mandated minimum prison terms is without parallel internationally, and no other nation imprisons the poor for their inability to pay fines for minor offenses.

The great costs—economic, social, political—of a failed criminal justice system are beyond dispute; they affect prisoners, their families (especially children), their communities and the public at large.

While acknowledging the problem, some commentators believe that the figures cited represent gross over-simplification, that some American jurisdictions have world-class prison educational and rehabilitation programs, and that international conditions differ so significantly that generalizations can be misleading.

The heart of the challenge is to determine what we can learn from those with the most effective criminal justice systems. Universal experience indicates that not revenge (punishment and public humiliation of malefactors), but crime prevention and rehabilitation of transgressors should be the goal. Basic education for those lacking it, vocational training opportunities, mental health and narcotic addiction services when appropriate and isolation for those few hardcore, intractable individuals who cannot be permitted to return to civilian society—these are what make a system work.

Too often in America, semi-literate high school dropouts, six times more likely to be imprisoned than high school graduates, leave jail no better educated than when they entered. With prison records that hinder employment and with no access to public housing or welfare programs, is it surprising that so many return to crime?

This is particularly true of those who have served time in private, for-profit prisons, currently a five billion dollar industry with large profits and no incentive to provide prisoners with other than minimal services.

Many of our elected officials believe they gain votes by being 'tough on crime.' The public cheers—influenced by our Calvinist tradition of punishment and public humiliation (e.g. Hawthorne's Hester Prynne forced to wear an "A" for adultery).

Only an informed citizenry can demand from national, state and local governments the best 21st century practices that will bring our criminal justice systems in line with the world's best. Rebuilding the troubled lives of former prisoners benefits all of society. Such an approach does not cost, it pays—in the form of a satisfied public and lower tax bills.

AMERICA'S IDENTITY CRISIS—
"WHAT AM I?" VS. "WHO AM I?"

The characteristics that distinguish us as individuals and those we share with others have become burning issues in American life. Stereotypic thinking today tries to place us in rigid categories that limit us, demean us and define us by the lowest common denominator of a dysfunctional group. In the process, everyone loses and we must battle such thinking.

Extremists seek to pigeonhole us simplistically, but we all have multiple, hybrid identities. The challenge is to relate to one another—regardless of background—in ways that encourage social cohesion. Multiple ethnicities and religious views, differing genders and sexual orientations and varying economic and educational levels are facts of life, as are our urban or rural, northern or southern, coastal or mid-nation backgrounds. But that should not preclude interactions with civility and respect for our mutual benefit.

It is human nature to feel more at ease with those like ourselves, more secure and less defensive. All human sub-groups need positive reinforcement of their self-image, assurance that they are recognized as human beings, respected as social participants and accepted for their values and outlook. Emotional and psychological well-being requires self-esteem, self-confidence and respect from others. Lack of it increases anxiety and depression, anger and hostility. In short, we need to feel comfortable with those like us and with those who differ from us.

An important challenge is to relate constructively to those who share with us one attribute—such as skin color, educational level, geographic regional outlook—without fighting with those who do not. We must work to make our sub-group membership a plus in our lives, not a minus.

Two conflicting approaches to inter-group relationships should be acknowledged. One, the "melting pot" theory, assumes that in due course all groups will sufficiently share fundamentals so as to permit peaceful and mutually-beneficial interactions. The other—the "salad bowl" or "mosaic" theory—assumes legal, political and economic equality of opportunity for all without sacrifice of any particular identity characteristic. (For example, forty percent of millennial American Jews tell pollsters that "having a sense of humor" is part of "being Jewish".)

The melting pot is represented by America's 19th Century poor Italian and Irish immigrants who were shunned by some, but whose descendants today constitute the American mainstream. The mosaic is exemplified by the Cherokee or Navajo mother who wants her child to live on a reservation, speak the native tongue and observe Native American lifestyles. A healthy American society can accommodate both.

Some problems have no easy answers. All Americans agree that no child should be denied the chance of equal socio-economic upward mobility because of parental limitations; on the other hand, we just do not know the extent to which, for example, a Muslim parent can justifiably control all aspects of her child's life (including female circumcision, childhood arranged marriages, the mandatory wearing of identity-hiding face veils), or the degree to which an Ultra-Orthodox Jew can preclude his child from receiving a secular education.

For the bulk of the public, heroes and role models from their own sub-group can help them seek productive and fulfilling positions in the American mainstream.

For disadvantaged inner-city minority teenagers, academic stars like Henry Louis Gates, Jr., generals like Colin Powell, diplomats like

Condoleezza Rice, world class scientists like Neil deGrasse Tyson, business titans like Kenneth Chenault or Richard Parsons and countless others can inspire, motivate and encourage efforts to follow their examples.

Today inner-city black elementary school children - with distinctive vocabularies, styles of self-expression, time sense and behavioral patterns—perform better academically with black role models and with teachers who understand and respect them. Enhancing a child's self-confidence, self-esteem and motivation to perform at the highest level of the child's ability gives that youngster a huge advantage in the drive for upward mobility. Stable home life—with paternal as well as maternal involvement—is an important plus factor for every child and it should be encouraged.

For mature people, reaching out beyond their comfort groups and seeking agreeable and constructive relationships with others is a worthwhile challenge. Broadening one's circle of friends, colleagues and acquaintances is intellectually stimulating, socially invigorating and professionally helpful.

America's founding motto "E pluribus unum" (out of many, one) conveys a vision of harmonious relationships and interactions between individuals despite their differences; and that vision—of individuals, not stereotypes—should prevail today.

All human institutions are subject to evolution and change, and those of us who believe in "American exceptionalism" are confident of our continuing progress. In the foreseeable future, we can make great strides toward a society reflecting the greatest good for the greatest number while making appropriate provision for those currently left behind.

The future-mindedness, fair play, pragmatism, compassion and public spiritedness required to achieve these aims would reflect the American ethos at its best. It is a goal toward which we must aspire.

FRESH THINKING ON SOCIAL CLASS

Economists, who tend to quantify everything, think of social class primarily in terms of income and wealth. Sociologists, who look beyond numbers, regard educational achievement and professional standing as key class indicators. Anthropologists, who observe how people think and act, consider hierarchies of social status and prestige and "who respects and disrespects whom."

Sophisticated observers in recent years have added "future-mindedness" as a crucial class determinant, differentiating those who are "broke" from those who are "poor."

Structural factors like the concentrated poverty in segregated, post-industrial inner-city neighborhoods are facts of life, as are the passed-along benefits that well-to-do educated parents – the so-called "dream hoarders"–provide for their children. In the real world, some from the socioeconomic bottom do rise and some from the top do fall. That often depends on their degree of future-mindedness, reflecting the culture in which they were raised.

J.D. Vance, in "Hillbilly Elegy," his study of the Appalachian poor, says, "What separates the successful from the unsuccessful are the expectations they had for their own lives…whenever people ask me what I'd like to change about the white working class, I say, "the feeling that our personal choices don't matter."

When Robert Merton coined the terms "self-fulfilling prophecy" and "role model" and when Edward Banfield stressed the importance of deferred gratification and long-term goals, they were anticipating the mindset of Asian students from economically-deprived backgrounds who went on to perform impressively in American high schools and colleges.

The Jewish grandmother in the old joke who identifies the twin babies she is tending as "this one is the doctor and that one is the lawyer" is influencing their future. And a questioning, self-disciplined youngster, whether in the Appalachian foothills or an inner-city ghetto, will achieve more if convinced that an advanced education is desirable and attainable. Luck has been defined as "an opportunity for which you are prepared," and when opportunity presents itself, these children will be able to take advantage of the luck we all need to meet life's challenges.

Structural problems (which are real) and personal agency (which can be influenced) must be faced; dealing with one and not the other is "necessary but not sufficient." The challenge to society is to provide appropriate educational and employment opportunities; the challenge to the individual is to take advantage of them.

All subgroups—regardless of skin color, ethnicity, geographic location, religion, etc.—reflect a bell curve of intelligence distribution in which the center is an I.Q. of 100. Those scoring 15 points below to those 15 points above represent 70% of the population, or the national average. About 2% of the public have I.Q.'s of 130 or higher.

If no significant intellectual accomplishment has ever been achieved by anyone raised in an igloo in Northern Alaska or on a Native American Blackfoot reservation in Montana (in which the unemployment rate today is 70%), think of the loss to America! A potential Leonardo DaVinci or an Isaac Newton born—with every possible handicap—would not be able to flower, and we would all lose.

Studies from Nobel Prize winner James Heckman and others document the crucial importance of a child's earliest years, when the basis for later development is established. Among the world's advanced nations, only the United States permits so high a number of our children to be raised without the basic skills, knowledge and attitudes necessary for productive and fulfilling lives in the modern world. The first 1,000 days are crucial, with home being the first school and parents the first teachers. It is in the first two to three years that a child's self-image is established, socialization with others is set, basic vocabulary mastered and thought patterns formed. Scholars Charles Murray and Robert Putnam (following Daniel Patrick Moynihan) cite differing attitudes toward marriage as important social class differentials which have profound impact on children. If a parent is unable to stimulate a child, other forces must be marshaled in loco parentis.

Other advanced nations—particularly the Nordic countries—have demonstrated the possibilities of a society with fewer socioeconomic contrasts and greater genuine equality of opportunity (and higher levels of health and happiness) than ours. We can learn from their examples, such as making higher education and effective vocational training more widely available.

Future-mindedness—and a mindset of self-discipline and high aspiration—are the keys to the upward mobility we wish to see available to all. We must inculcate them early in life. Achieved later, this will be a higher cost, for fewer people and with greater difficulty.

However it can be done, and some outstanding examples show the way. The Harlem Educational Activities Fund (HEAF), New York's renowned afterschool program for inner-city public high school students, has always inculcated future-mindedness and high aspirations in its students. That is reflected in HEAF's 100% public high school graduation rate, with nearly 100% of its students going on to four-year colleges. Nationwide, 11% of all U.S. high school students go on to graduate school, while HEAF's rate is some 35%. There are no tests to join their program, only an eagerness to learn.

Universal experience has shown clear lessons. Stable two-parent homes, effective pre-school and elementary educations, the cultivation of high aspiration and—yes, future-mindedness—are the chief factors in upward mobility and in a fulfilling life. Our post World War II G.I. Bill demonstrated that available college education for those who qualify is an excellent national investment that pays rather than a "private consumer good that costs."

It would be a stroke of national good fortune to have these questions discussed and debated in the forthcoming presidential election.

SHOULD UNDERGRADUATES STUDY HISTORY?

With short-term vocational training displacing humanities studies at colleges across the country, advocates of traditional education are on the defensive: Why waste a student's time—and tuition dollars—on activities of no immediate use and little interest to potential employers?

The transmission of substantive knowledge and insights, the acquisition of skill in reading difficult texts, and the inculcation of values—leading to the ability to make sound judgments—are seen increasingly as appropriate only for academics.

There is no longer agreement that the ability to make better judgments applies to every area of life – to each of us as a voting citizen, as an employer or employee, as an individual seeking a fulfilling life. We no longer agree that knowledge of the past and of the experiences of our predecessors will help us deal more effectively with the challenges of the present and future.

What does Thucydides, the Athenian general and historian, tell us about America's failed strategies in Iraq and Iran? What would Sun Tzu, ancient China's author of "The Art of War," think of our involvement in Afghanistan? How would Machiavelli suggest we deal with a rising China, a failing Russia and a static Japan? What does Admiral Alfred Thayer Mahan, the leading American strategist of the 19th century, tell us about China's designs on key Pacific Islands? How do General von Clausewitz's views bear on North Korea's nuclear threat?

Thinkers long gone can help us with today's challenges. Of course history does not repeat itself exactly. Given the number of differing factors, we should only seek generalizations from the past that stimulate present thinking.

Does the Dutch Tulip Craze in 17th Century Holland teach us only about over-valued flowers? Does the Wall Street crash of 1929 tell us only about over-valued common stocks? Does Japan's trauma in 1989 over inflated land prices tell us only about Asian urban problems? I considered them all when, in the Spring of 2008, the editor of The Wharton Journal asked me for an essay on then current economic prospects.

My outlook was grim, given the ten million families with over-financed homes of below-zero equity value. The Fall 2008 issue of The Wharton Journal, containing my piece warning of a real estate bubble, appeared on September 1st. On September 11th, I received a complimentary letter about it from Paul Volcker. On September 15th, Lehman Brothers declared bankruptcy and economic chaos followed. History did not repeat itself in detail, but it did in concept.

History teaches us about the present by explaining how it evolved from the past. It teaches us how people and societies once behaved and may behave again. The study of history gives us the skills necessary for assessing evidence and for evaluating competing interpretations. It teaches us the relationship between theory and practice and it teaches us to question our preconceptions and those of others.

The study of history also gives insights into leadership mentalities. Harry Truman told his biographers that he had learned more about politics from Plutarch's Lives than from any treatise on political science. Some observers today feel that a study of the Roman Emperor Commodus (son of Marcus Aurelius) might explain the motives of our current President; others suggest parallels to Kaiser Wilhelm II.

In an age of nuclear and biological weapons, the stakes are higher than ever. The resolution of past confrontations can prepare us for our present problems. Our leaders today would do well to ponder the adage of Sun Tzu – "The supreme art of war is to subdue the enemy without fighting," a concept as valid today as it was in fifth century B.C. China.

At the moment, our public—and our educators—do not seem to value the study of history. Let us hope that in due course—along with civil political discourse, an interest in objective facts and an appreciation of the expertise of trained specialists—the value of historical study will again be recognized.

HERACLITUS AND 21ST CENTURY AMERICAN JUDAISM

The ancient Greek philosopher Heraclitus observed that one cannot step into the same river twice, since the river keeps changing and you keep changing. His insight applies today to American Judaism, which evolves in its own way just as American society undergoes transformation.

Generational changes in American attitudes and values today are apparent in many ways, including diminishing national engagement with organized religion.

Thirty-five percent of Millennials (Americans born between 1981 and 1996) are religiously unaffiliated today, compared with 17% of Baby Boomers (born 1946-1964) and 11% of the Silent Generation (born 1928-1945). Self-described Protestants have dropped in number today from 22% of the old to 11% of the young, and Roman Catholics from 24% of the old to 16% of the young. Financial contributions to the Catholic church have dropped precipitously, and, while the Church remains resolutely anti-birth control, few Catholic families today have more than two or three children. Episcopal Church membership and attendance keep dropping, and in the past decade some 10% of Episcopal parishes and missions have closed. Presbyterians today number 1.4 million, down from 2.8 million in 1960.

America's six million-plus Jews are a special case because of their historical experiences and memories, the broad spectrum of their theological beliefs and ritual observance, their diverse demographics and their complex emotional bonds to Israel. Among the Jewish young, 94% tell pollsters they are "proud of being Jewish," although over half have no formal identification with Jewish institutions. Well over half choose non-Jewish spouses and over half describe themselves as Jews by culture rather than by theology.

The challenge for the American Jewish community is to deal constructively with this broad spectrum of belief and observance today, ranging from those traditional believers called "tribalists" to those modernists known as "covenantors".

Tribalists see Judaism in theological, ethnic and political terms, considering Jews a Chosen People following rules of conduct laid down in the Torah or Talmud. They are explicit in denominational loyalty and religious practice and are concerned with Jewish communal continuity and survival. Identification with Israel and Holocaust memorialization are important to them.

Covenantors, on the other hand, regard Judaism in ethical and moral terms, as a spiritual legacy with a humanistic culture reflecting social justice, without necessary reference to a Supreme Being or personal deity. The Bible is respected as wisdom literature, and holidays and life-cycle ceremonies are seen as symbolic expressions of spirituality and wisdom. And they respond to the exhortation in the Book of Micah 6:8, "What doth the Lord require of thee but to do justly, to love mercy and to walk humbly with thy God."

A healthy, pluralistic American Jewish community must make room for all its members (10% of whom are Orthodox, 18% Conservative, 35% Reform, 6% Reconstructionist and other, 30% of no denomination). In a period of declining attendance and membership in synagogues and temples, of diminishing financial contributions to Jewish Federations and of weakening Jewish institutions, an increasing number of young Jews feed their spiritual hunger at yoga centers and ashrams, with personal gurus and meditation training and through public non-religious social welfare activities.

The implication for the future of Jewish life in America evokes varied responses. One—that of the tribalists— is for the organized Jewish community to continue its present course, with most rabbis opposing intermarriage, highlighting denominational differences and turning a blind eye to the Israeli government's open disparagement of non-Orthodox Judaism (which increasingly alienates young Americans).

A more realistic response is to acknowledge the broad range of Jewish belief, with those self-identifying as Jews encouraged to raise their children as knowledgeable and involved members of the Jewish community, proud of its past and enthusiastic about its future. Jews by culture see themselves not as a "Chosen People" but as "choosing people," who identify with Judaism through volition, not just by maternal descent or formal conversion.

Whether Jewish by theology or culture, all can find the soul-searching and introspection of the High Holy Days life-enhancing; they can delight in the joyous celebration of freedom of the Passover Seder, and in the weekly Sabbath dinner's expression of gratitude for all those good things in our lives not of our own doing.

Jews-by-culture generally list several life-enhancing convictions that all Jews share:

A) All Jews relate in some ways to other Jews. The individual is not considered in isolation but in a context of home, family, community and society. Observant Jews pray in a minyan, but all can celebrate the Sabbath dinner with family and friends, celebrate the Passover Seder with a multi-generational gathering including strangers, the needy and non-Jewish friends.

B) Lifelong learning and endless questioning are important values. "Rabbi Hillel says this, Rabbi Shamai says that. What do you think?"

C) Philanthropy is not seen as reflecting charity (based on "caritas" or love) but as "tzedakah" (based on justice). Martin Luther King Jr. said that some 90% of the major contributions he received for the

Southern Christian Leadership Conference came from Jews, and he admired the role Julius Rosenwald played in establishing 5,000 black schools in the American south. "Tzedakah" rather than "caritas."

D) All religions acknowledge the world's Creator. Only Judaism, in the doctrine of "tikkun olam," maintains that the world was deliberately left incomplete so that each of us could help repair or finish it.

E) Finally, Jews-by-culture feel that Judaism, while not proselytizing, should be open to all who choose to be affiliated.

In this view, intermarried non-Jewish spouses, their children and their families should be welcome at Sabbath dinners, Passover Seders and Purim Balls. Continuing efforts should be made to increase the knowledge and understanding of Judaism of all Jews, whether of maternal descent or not. Interdenominational entities like Hillel International and the JCCA (Jewish Community Center Association) play an important role in maintaining constructive relationships among members of the broad spectrum of Jewish belief and observance.

America's Jewish communities of the future can flourish, but they will differ in form and content from the past. Not blood lines, but intellectual and spiritual concerns will bind the members; not tribal loyalties, but shared values; not observance of religious rituals, but performance of life-enhancing and socially constructive activities. And the new covenant will be open to all who wish to join.

Chinese Confucians particularly may be receptive to Judaism by choice, as they learn of Hillel's response to the cynic who asked for the essential message of Judaism while he stood on one foot (Shabbat 31a). Hillel's reply has resounded through the ages: "Do not do unto others what you do not want them to do unto you. That is the whole of the Torah, the rest is commentary. Go now and study."

In our present age of fear and negativism, the Jewish message of hope and its embrace of what the ancient Greeks called eudaimonia (happiness from meaning and purpose in life and identification with goals larger than ourselves) will appeal to many. Our challenge is to encourage the intermarried to think of themselves as part of the Jewish community.

A healthy Jewish community can include the Ultra-Orthodox, Modern Orthodox, Conservative, Reform, Reconstructionist and others less doctrinaire, if we will it. As Rabbi Jonathan Sacks has written, "On all matters that affect us as Jews we work together regardless of our religious differences; on all things that touch on our religious differences we agree to differ, but with respect."

As the Book of Proverbs says, "A good doctrine has been given unto you. Forsake it not."

April 23, 2019

EVOLVING CITIES – DEMOGRAPHICALLY, ECONOMICALLY, PHYSICALLY

From their earliest origins, cities have evolved to meet the emerging needs of the societies they served. Whether as trading or production centers, military bastions, administrative headquarters or entertainment and cultural repositories, cities change as conditions change.

The technological, social and demographic factors we face today will be reflected in adaptations in our urban settings, just as Henry Ford's 1913 introduction of the assembly line or the many 19th century immigrants changed our cities in the past; and the sooner we prepare for new emerging factors, the better.

Although the micro and macro factors influencing the life and character of cities differ, worldwide experience today demonstrates that local pragmatists, rather than nationalist ideologues, are better at problem-solving, and that innovative change in a city is more apt to come from the bottom up. The effective interaction of local businesses, philanthropies, colleges and cultural institutions is the hallmark of civic vitality, and competent leadership can harness it to address emerging problems.

The shift of retail purchasing from local stores to the internet; the increasing number of young people living at home with parents; the changing balance between home purchasing and renting; and the flight of middle class children from failing inner city schools are already apparent. They will be reflected in recycled shopping malls and industrial buildings; better intra-regional transportation; taller buildings with higher urban densities, smaller room sizes and more amenities; more transient and fewer permanent accommodations; and a re-thinking of property taxation, changing the balance of the burden from rental housing toward one family homes.

In brick-and-mortar matters, cities need both the Robert Moses and the Jane Jacobs approach—efficient transportation systems but also livable communities with individual character and a sense of place.

Of macro factors, the impact of 3-D printing, self-driving trucks and buses, and automation's replacement of many clerical jobs will be reflected in a lessened need for labor; and the ramifications will be profound. How should we occupy the time, provide the sense of self-respect and what Thorstein Veblen called "pride of craftsmanship"—let alone provide a living income for all? It will demand our best thinking.

To meet the challenges—for the future of our cities and for the national quality of life—we need more effective deliberation than we have today, especially on the macro factors.

Unfortunately, voters today demand more services and benefits than they are willing to pay for in taxes, sacrificing the long term for the short term; and pandering politicians encourage that choice. Deteriorating infrastructure, disgraceful educational results and shorter life expectancies for the poor are the inevitable immediate results, with social upheaval a possible future prospect for a society that keeps hoping for a "free lunch" instead of rational trade-offs.

How do we reverse those trends, when fanatics from the extreme political right and left dominate public discourse and the "vital center" whispers ineffectually to itself? As Harvard's Robert Putnam says, we need less "red" or "blue" thinking and more "purple."

Continuity and change are facts of life. Conservative centrists focus more on keeping the best of the old, while liberal centrists focus more on encouraging the best of the new; but both sides of the centrist world value informed civil debate, consensus-seeking and sensible compromise. The prudent people in the middle must make themselves heard. And they must demand leaders of character and competence, knowledge and experience, who take pride in good performance and shame in bad.

Politics and government cannot continue to be a "spectator sport." We all must re-think what economists call the public's "source and application of funds"—what revenues, from what sources, to be raised how, to be spent by whom, on what means toward what ends? What proportion of our gross expenditures should be by individuals for private choices, and what proportion for public goods available to everyone? What should we consume today and what do we owe to the future? What are our obligations to those who, for whatever reason, cannot produce and have needs for which they cannot pay?

The questions are clear, the answers less so; and social scientists today are appropriately modest in their assertions. After their blatant failure to anticipate either the economic meltdown of 2009 or the results of the 2016 Presidential election, their failure to predict either the dramatic national increase in crime in the 1970's or its recent dramatic decline, the public has lost confidence in "expertise" and forecasters are humble. They recall Winston Churchill's comment about a political opponent, Clement Attlee—"a modest man with much to be modest about."

Still, we must try, with all the wisdom we can muster and with all we can learn from the experiences of other advanced nations. In a period when the "new normal" is likely to reflect lower rates of economic growth than in the past, we must husband our resources more astutely than ever, with appropriate incentives for actions conducive to the public good and disincentives for the bad.

With appropriate modesty, I hazard suggestions that may be helpful on four factors that influence both the physical and psychological quality of life in our cities: infrastructure, taxation, education and health care.

Deteriorating infrastructure, our most pressing problem, is open to straight-forward resolution. In a period of low interest rates and adequate savings, long term state bonds financed by automotive user fees such as on mileage and higher user tolls for roads and bridges seem self-evident. Water resources, sewage facilities, dams and nuclear facilities must be planned and financed with long term perspectives, for which many economists recommend a carbon tax (both to raise revenue and to influence consumption).

Addressing our over-regulated economy is an important first step in dealing with infrastructure, as we acknowledge that major highway improvements that take one year in Germany and two years in Canada usually take some eight years in the U.S., because of overlapping jurisdictions and poor coordination. Appropriate Congressional review of our regulatory climate with indicated reforms (requiring cost-benefit analysis and transparency in debate) could improve the regulation of infrastructure improvement considerably.

Taxation is a more controversial question, since efforts to raise revenue face the protest that higher personal income taxes, corporate taxes or estate taxes are counter-productive; and the challenge is to find the least harmful form of revenue production. Virtually all other advanced economies find that taxes on consumption, through a Value Added Tax (V.A.T.), are the most effective form of taxation. With exemptions for food and rent, health care and education (which reflect the bulk of expenditures of the poor), consumption taxes are the least onerous source of government revenue.

Corporate and personal taxes should relate rationally to the tax levels of other nations, and the current U.S. corporate rate of 35% needs reconsideration. But we do need more national revenue to pay for the services and benefits demanded by the aging publics of advanced nations in the 21st century. Cutting expenses by raising age levels for social security and other age-related benefits is recommended by some economists, but it may not be politically feasible.

Education is a topic on which our national views are bewildering. Experience shows that education does not "cost" but that it "pays" for society at large. The classic demonstration was the study of identical twins and the post-World War II G.I. Bill, which established free college tuition for veterans. The higher income taxes and estate taxes paid by the college-educated twin gave the government a huge return on its educational investment. Similarly, experience shows that school dropouts "cost" society while high school and college graduates "pay." And the payment is not only financial but social, as our cities become safer and more civilized for all of us in every way.

A sensitive point about education involves the poor showing on objective tests that our public high school students make in comparison with those of other advanced nations, such as the Nordic countries. The key factors are two: teachers and students. Their teachers come from the top 10% of the national education pool, are well-trained, highly paid and universally respected and they are promoted on merit, not longevity. Their students are well-prepared to do high school level work. (As the Good Book says, "Go thou and do likewise.")

On the current debate about equality, commonsense says that true "equality of result" is not in the real world; but "equality of opportunity," a much more level playing field, could be achievable if we want it and are willing to pay for it, through better educational services for the young or disadvantaged and life-long educational and vocational programs for all. A more meritocratic, and more productive, society would result.

For our health care that is poor by the standards of other advanced nations, the U.S. spends 16.9% of its GDP, while the U.K. spends 9.8%, France 11.1% and Germany 11.2%. Wiser, more efficient U.S. health care services are clearly the answer, with our health care professionals called upon to think more of the Hippocratic Oath than of the current mantra, "What the traffic will bear."

In short, the quality of life in our cities and in our society will be determined by the difficult choices we make and the means we use to implement them. Science and technology are solving the age old problem of subsistence. It is up to us to create the context conducive to lives that are productive and fulfilling.

In ancient Greece, young Athenians, on achieving full citizenship, took what was called the Ephebic Oath. They pledged to transmit their city to the future enhanced if possible but in no way diminished. That is a goal we should share.

Bryn Mawr College
May 26, 2017

THE HARLEM TIMES EDITORIALS

YOUR CHILD, THE GENIUS

The great Polish musician Paderewski was hailed by an admirer with the cry, "You are a genius!" "Yes, I am," the maestro replied, "but before I became a genius I was a drudge."

Drudgery – intense, sustained, unremitting effort, sharply focused on long term goals – is not the sole factor in making your child a genius, but it dramatically improves the odds.

Current knowledge, experience and professional beliefs agree on the factors – including natural ability – that are involved in a child's high achievement later in life. And the earlier they come into play, the more effective their impact.

One of the most important – and least discussed – is the 'self-fulfilling prophecy' of high expectations held by a child's family. Those who assume their child can be a high achiever must act on that assumption from the child's birth. Hugging, kissing, cuddling; singing, playing games, telling and reading stories – all stimulate a baby's development. Well before a child enters kindergarten – whether through home efforts or pre-school programs – the child should be able to speak clearly; recognize letters and numbers, and have a basic vocabulary. Presumably the child has also been socialized to play with other children and to follow a teacher's instructions.

Once in kindergarten, natural curiosity and previous exposure to stories should result in the child's readiness to learn to read. Continued reading to the child – at home or in school – of simple books (with praise for the child's initial reading efforts) will be reflected in the child's ability to read at grade level.

At this point, the quality of the school experience becomes a major factor. Throughout elementary and junior high school, our "genius to be" should become increasingly self-motivated and future-minded. First rate teachers – well-trained, well-equipped, with high expectations for their pupils – are crucial. An environment conducive to learning is another key factor – safe, orderly classrooms, appropriate libraries and computers, etc. and fellow students eager to learn are the ideal.

The goal of admission to a first rate high school – public or private – is self-evident. Admissions test preparation – whether through on-line activities like Kumon or through programs like Kaplan – are worth the effort and, if possible, parental expense.

Class size, the physical condition of the school building, the income level of the parents, the pay scale of the teachers and the degree of demographic diversity are sometimes demanded, but one should recall the history of N.Y.'s City College Class of 1937. In the history of Nobel Prizes, this was the only undergraduate class to produce three Nobel Laureates. Yet City College in 1937 had large classes in shabby buildings taught by underpaid academics to an undiversified student body with desperately poor parents. The superb quality of teaching in an atmosphere of fierce student motivation and high aspirations resembled that of Stuyvesant High School or Bronx High School of Science today.

Conclusion:

To produce your 'genius,' assume the child's high potential from birth. Encourage the work habits of a drudge and the aspirations of a winner. Demand excellent teachers and fight for a school atmosphere conducive to learning, Then stand back and cheer!

July, 2014

THE COMMUNITY ROLE IN EDUCATION

Statistics on inner city student low achievement rates – from preschool reading scores through college graduation rates – are heart-breaking.

The causes are well-known. They range from structural challenges that are economic or political, through social ones like racism or negative peer pressure, to personal agency ones such as lack of student self-confidence, low motivation or an inability to apply sustained, self-disciplined effort.

Structural and social reasons for low inner city achievement are profound. They must be fought – at all times, by everyone and by all feasible means. The personal agency problem is more complex, influenced as it is by many factors. Its solution involves fresh thinking by everyone, but especially by community leaders.

Those leaders – politicians, ministers, social workers and educators – must acknowledge the inability of the public school system and of many families to meet the needs of inner city children. Those educational, emotional, social and psychological needs can be met in part by programs conducted by Harlem churches, community groups, social clubs, P.T.A.'s and so forth.

In China, orphan asylums are often located near old age retirement homes so that the elderly can read, play with, stimulate and encourage youngsters. China does not have a patent on the concept and it can be modified for the benefit of Harlem children.

The importance of a child's earliest years – especially from birth through age five – is universally recognized. Adult involvement – helping with reading readiness and vocabulary, strengthening a child's sense of self-esteem and high motivation – has life-long impact.

Giving Kids a Fair Chance, the new book by Nobel Prize winner James Heckman, makes the point clearly. "Skill begets skill, motivation begets motivation; and the benefits of later interventions are greatly enhanced by earliest interventions." Conversely, a child who is behind his peers at the start of kindergarten is hard-pressed to catch up, and a child who is behind in the fourth grade is unlikely ever to catch up.

Volunteer groups from every church could be organized to give elderly retirees a vehicle encouraging them to read to or speak with young children, accompany them on visits to museums or help the children understand that they are important, that someone cares about them, that they count. The increased vocabulary, the realization that reading can be enjoyable and helpful, and the enlarged vision of the world the children receive can change their lives.

At the elementary school level, all children should be exposed to supportive adults, whether family members or others, who praise their accomplishments, sympathize with their setbacks and encourage them to keep trying.

At the high school level, youngsters should be helped outside the classroom to study in groups, to practice public speaking, to interact positively with grownups, to relate to those who encourage their aspirations.

As college beckons, in the black world, as in the Asian-American world, sympathetic adults should help students prepare for admission tests, selection of colleges, applications for scholarships, etc.

For young people not ready, able or willing to go on with formal education, industrial or commercial vocational training programs should be available for a wide variety of trades and occupations where those young people can acquire the skills and knowledge that will enable them to lead productive and satisfying lives.

The U.S. military conducts one of the world's great vocational training institutions, and military veterans can advise and encourage inner city youngsters to enlist in the military to learn skills and receive on-the-job training that will prove invaluable in their after-service careers.

Online self-education opportunities are available to all, and older volunteers can help inner city youngsters to use them effectively.

Every child should be encouraged to realize his or her full potential.

"It takes a village to raise a child," says the African proverb – in addition to, not instead of, a supportive family environment. If the family environment is not adequate, the community should meet those needs.

The biblical response to the ancient question, "Am I my brother's keeper?" is an unequivocal "yes." By extension, the entire community should accept responsibility for the social, intellectual and moral growth of its children.

July, 2014

HI TECH AND BLACK EMPLOYMENT

A brute fact of life in 2014 is that black inner city youth are being frozen out of lucrative future high tech careers for lack of early preparation in mathematics. In addition to—not instead of—reading, writing and speaking effectively, early mastery of the basic computation skills is crucial to a child's future educational development.

Children who fall behind by the fourth grade rarely catch up. Pundits who bemoan the under-representation of black engineers, computer technicians, even C.P.A.s must look first at the state of elementary schooling.

These are the years when the child's self-confidence in the ability to perform successfully is internalized, when their view of the world and of life goals and aspirations are established. Negative stereotypic thinking about black children, lack of classroom stimulus or preparation, negative peer pressure, lack of encouragement or example by family or neighbors destroy the prospects of countless inner city children capable of significant accomplishment.

The failure of the New York City public education system to instill in children in their earliest years basic arithmetic proficiency required for later math progress must be acknowledged. The question is what parents or the wider community can do to help those children prepare for the more advanced mathematics required for an increasing percentage of meaningful careers.

All mathematics is hierarchical, with proficiency in addition, subtraction, multiplication and division of whole numbers (then of fractions and decimals) the foundation of the geometry and algebra that should be mastered in elementary and junior high school.

Parents and community institutions must fill the gap between what the child needs and what the school provides. Through books, stories, games and toys; building blocks, exposure to cooking recipes or baseball batting averages, children should be encouraged to feel that numbers are important and understandable and that dealing with them can be fun. Thinking of fractions through examples such as a pizza pie divided into halves or quarters, or figuring how many pennies buy a candy bar or make change in a purchase, telling time and determining how many hours until supper—helps preschoolers prepare for "the next step."

Children whose parents or other adults check their geometry or algebra homework and praise their efforts and success are being prepared for the calculus study that will be crucial for college admissions and later careers.

The heartbreaking number of youngsters who drop out of high school or who enter college requiring many remedial courses is a charge against our society. That blacks constitute 12% of the U.S. population but receive 7% of STEM bachelor's degrees, 4% of master's degrees and 2% of Ph.D.'s are challenges that must be faced. If only 3% of U.S. high school students in Advanced Placement classes are black, is it surprising that later numbers are bleak?

Inner city children must understand that negative cultural stereotypes do not apply to them, and they must take heart from the knowledge that the world-class astrophysicist Neil deGrasse Tyson was advised by his high school teacher to pursue a career in sports rather than in science!

Bright, ambitious inner city students should stretch to prepare for Advanced Placement (AP) and college prep classes that are important for admission to colleges and universities; they must avail themselves of summer school and after-school programs; they must look ahead and prepare today for exhilarating, productive careers of tomorrow.

America's national interest requires all the talented, well-trained innovators and creators we can produce, regardless of skin color. It is in the national interest to see that talented inner city youngsters are in the pipeline.

Self-disciplined, sustained effort; future-mindedness and the planning that goes with it; self-confidence based on a previous record of accomplishment—these are the assets inner city children must be able to bring to the table. If they seek a motto, it can be that of the victorious sailors with Aeneas in ancient Rome: "They were able because they thought they were able!"

November 2014

TA-NEHISI COATES—
LOOKING BACKWARD OR FORWARD?

Ta-Nehisi Coates is widely acknowledged as one of the nation's most eloquent, powerful journalists. The passion, knowledge and command of language he brings to discussions of the state of Black America are compelling; and his latest book, *Between the World and Me*, is a thought-provoking intellectual challenge for all Americans.

In the form of a letter to his 14-year-old son, Samori, it conveys the soul-destroying nature of American slavery, of Jim Crow segregation, and of the vicious impact of anti-black racism and prejudice to this very day. Racism, like homophobia, sexism and anti-Semitism, continues to plague us and it must be acknowledged. It is destructive and it must be fought by those impatient to see American society live up to its high ideals.

Coates conveys legitimate demands for compassion and understanding with great power and clarity. But a separate question arises from Coates' message to his son's generation. On that, objective observers can disagree. Many fear that Coates' negativism, lack of hope, and his failure to acknowledge the social progress our society has made on issues of race and racism in recent years send a counter-productive message to young African Americans of every class who need to know how much progress our society has made and is making. This should encourage them to aspire to reach their full potential and to overcome any obstacles they may face.

Since the U.S. Civil War, black thinkers have been of at least two-minds—"separatists" (like Marcus Garvey) who looked with despair upon American society and who believed that anti-black racism would always be with us, and "integrationists" who looked forward with hope to black inclusiveness without reservation. The latter view was best expressed by Martin Luther King Jr.'s comment that his children should be judged "not by the color of their skin but by the content of their character."

In his farewell speech to the nation, President Barack Obama noted that "race remains a potent and divisive force in our society ... we are not where we need to be ... going forward we must uphold the laws against discrimination in housing, in education, in employment and in the criminal justice system." President Obama ended with a plea to rebuild our institutions, but above all for personal agency and participation free of any internalized sense of limitation.

Objective reports of progress in racial social justice abound. The Pew Foundation notes the growing percentage of black students completing high school and college (now up to 23% of all black people aged 25 and older) and the current 47 black Congressional Representatives and three Senators (up from 13 in 1971). And the percentage of black generals, admirals, ambassadors, college presidents and millionaires in our country keeps increasing. In fact, since Dr. King was so tragically assassinated, the size of the black upper middle class has quadrupled.

Harvard professor Martin Kilson, in "Transformation of the African American Intelligentsia," today sees our black President as part of "a full-fledged African American political class made up of ten thousand elected office holders in counties, state legislatures and Congress and over 20,000 more African American administrative and technical officials at state and federal levels, with nearly four million African Americans recorded by U.S. Census Bureau surveys in 2002 and 2006 as holding top-tier white collar occupations."

In *Between the World and Me*, Coates is curiously ambivalent about the prospects for racial progress. At one point, he instills in his son debilitating fear of the police and distrust of all social authority; yet elsewhere he points out that he, himself, at age 14, did not know "what it means to grow up with a black President, social networks, omnipresent media and black women everywhere in their natural hair."

Coates conveys to his son the impression of black life as the product of forces beyond black control (implying the lack of personal responsibility) and he objects to the thought that blacks have to be "twice as good as whites" (removing the "challenge and response" mindset that has traditionally stimulated other minorities to rise within American society).

Coates also ignores encouraging reports such as that from the Brookings Institution that today blacks who graduate from high school, have a full-time job, don't have a child before age 21, and marry before child-bearing, have a 75% chance of attaining middle class status.

Coates says he was inspired to write his latest volume after re-reading James Baldwin's "The Fire Next Time," which was originally published in 1963 as a letter to Baldwin's 15 year old nephew. But Baldwin repeatedly implores his nephew to believe that revolutionary change is possible against all odds and that blacks should defeat the expectations of those who seek to control and exploit them.

One view of Coates' book (that of Michelle Alexander) is that, "Coates' book is unfinished. He raises numerous critically important questions that are unanswered ... I suppose that he is holding out on us. Everything he has ever written leads me to believe that he has more to say." One looks forward to the day when Coates feels comfortable enough to write about the great triumph that his own life represents as part of a larger generational phenomenon.

In an interview on the publication of the book, Coates described his idea of integration as "looking at little black girls and little white girls and not seeing any difference." Many of us believe that day may arrive well before Coates thinks possible and that by galvanizing constructive 'self-fulfilling prophecies' of high achievement we may speed the day.

At some point, the American public will accept the fact that "race" is essentially a social construct with what Anthony Appiah calls "imaginary natural commonalities," and we must work toward the day when "the ideal of human brotherhood has become a practical possibility." (W.E.B. DuBois)

March/April 2017

ON HEROES AND HERO-WORSHIP – COMMEMORATING W.E.B. DUBOIS

William Edward Burghardt DuBois (1868-1963) was the most prominent and influential black in American history. A spell-binding orator, prolific author and dynamic political activist, he spoke for and to America's black public as no one else before or since.

As a founder of the NAACP in 1909 and as crusading editor of its journal "The Crisis," he fought for full civil rights and increased political representation for blacks. He believed firmly that equal educational opportunity and achievement were the keys to racial integration and black advancement and that the leadership role of an educated "Talented Tenth" was critical to achievement in culture and social progress. Himself a cum laude graduate of Harvard University and its first African American to earn a Ph.D., he actively supported The Great Migration, helping blacks escape Southern racism and find economic opportunities elsewhere; DuBois' efforts helped over 600 blacks become U.S. Army officers in 1917.

For the next half century, DuBois wrote, spoke and conferred vigorously, fighting to outlaw lynching, to support women's rights and to permit inter-racial marriage. He battled for racial integration and against Marcus Garvey's endorsement of racial separation and he proclaimed Booker T. Washington's drive for low level vocational training "necessary but not sufficient" for true black advancement. He supported the artistic Harlem Renaissance in the 1920's, and in the

1930's he was horrified by German treatment of Jews, which he described as "an attack on civilization, comparable only to such horrors as the Spanish Inquisition or the African slave trade."

A life-long anti-war activist, he opposed U.S. intervention in World War II and the Korean War, and in 1950, as Chairman of the Peace Information Center, he fought to ban all nuclear weapons. The U.S. government alleged that the P.I.C. was an agent of a foreign state (for supporting the Stockholm Peace Appeal) and indicted DuBois, but the case was dismissed when the defense attorney told the judge that Dr. Albert Einstein had offered to appear as a character witness for Dr. DuBois.

An active supporter of Pan-African movements, he became friendly with Kwame Nkrumah, the future first President of Ghana, who invited him to Africa. While visiting Ghana in 1960, DuBois spoke with its then President about the creation of a new encyclopedia of the African diaspora, the "Encyclopedia Africana," and of establishing an international center and "think tank" to examine pan-African problems of education, health and sound democratic political institutions. In October 1961, at 93, DuBois and his wife moved to Ghana, bringing with them his extensive personal library and his voluminous personal papers. DuBois died on August 27, 1963 in Accra at the age of 95. The day after his death, at the March on Washington, the 250,000 participants were asked to observe a moment of silence in his honor.

Today, DuBois' childhood home in Great Barrington, Massachusetts is a National Historic Monument; two U.S. postage stamps carry his portrait; the main library of the University of Massachusetts Amherst is named after him as is the physics building at Fisk University. In due course, "Africana: The Encyclopedia of the African and African-American Experience" appeared, dedicated to DuBois by its editors, Kwame Anthony Appiah and Henry Louis Gates, Jr.

Sadly, the DuBois Center in Accra, Ghana has fallen into appalling deterioration and is in dire need, not only of a physical restoration and refurbishment, but of a total reconstitution of its management and support. A new International Board of Trustees is indicated, composed of prominent and eminent Ghanaians along with appropriate international figures; and sophisticated long-term planning is called for to protect and to revitalize what could and should become a major international project honoring this distinguished individual.

The Helping Africa Foundation, an American 501 (c)(3) philanthropic entity created by Kwame Anthony Appiah, Henry Louis Gates, Jr., Daniel Rose and others has undertaken to work with the government of Ghana in exploring ways of resuscitating this worthwhile project. Those interested in learning more about the proposed program are encouraged to contact the H.A.F.'s Executive Director Japhet Aryiku, who can be reached at: japhet@helpingafrica.org.

September 2017

AMAZON, GENTRIFICATION AND SILICON VALLEY EAST

"Gentrification" is the term widely applied to an influx of affluent young professionals displacing long-term lower-income residents and businesses in a revitalizing, dynamic urban setting.

Every European capital—and American cities like San Francisco, Atlanta, Baltimore, Seattle and Washington, D.C.—has witnessed tensions when newcomers cause property values to rise and rents increase, changing the character of a neighborhood. Thoughtful local leaders take prudent steps to ease some burdens on previous residents, but in no case—repeat, in no case—do responsible leaders turn their backs on major economic development substantially benefitting the greater public.

In the case of Amazon's proposed move to Long Island City—which would reinforce New York's claim to be the nation's second leading center of high tech innovation—the anticipated 25,000-plus new high-tech jobs (plus tens of thousands of others) and the $27 billion in projected long-term tax revenues are a more than sufficient New York financial incentive to justify the proposed $3 billion in incentives Amazon would receive, especially since those tax breaks are specifically dependent on job creation. This would be in addition to the construction jobs involved in building 4 million square feet of new office space.

New York's black community would clearly have benefited from Amazon's headquarters move, and the publicity-seeking politicians who were proud of killing the deal were selfishly working against the best interests of the minority world.

The complex positive feedback from such innovative high-tech development—ranging from increased purchasing power for upscale goods and services to increasing demand (and support) for varied cultural activities—can be dramatic. Lower crime rates and public pressure for better schools, hospitals and transit facilities usually follow.

Amazon's proposed new center in New York would be a win/win game. The pro-Amazon case should normally have been self-evident, but the inept, secretive manner in which negotiations were handled gave some local demagogues—outraged at not having been party to them—an excuse to incite opposition. One, a city councilman, attacks Amazon as anti-union; another, a state senator, attacks the financial arrangements. A third, a publicity-seeking U.S. Congresswoman, seeks to enhance her anti-capitalist credentials.

Fortunately, latest polls show that two-thirds of state-wide voters support the project, as do city voters, including residents of nearby Queensbridge Houses, the nation's largest public housing development. If Amazon would belatedly make clear the wide array of educational, vocational and social service programs it planned to sponsor (including exciting high-tech training activities with the new Cornell Tech campus on Roosevelt Island), these figures would presumably increase further.

The prospects could be exciting, and the likelihood would be good that New York could enhance its claim to be a leading world-class high-tech innovation center.

Globalization and rapidly evolving new technologies are facts of life—the challenge is to encourage their obvious benefits to be widely distributed through well-thought out business regulation, fair taxation and badly-needed greater public expenditure on education, health and mass transit.

Let's not kill the Goose; just pay better attention to how the Golden Eggs are divided! Perhaps negotiations can still be re-opened in a manner that makes clear that all can win.

March 2019

FUTURE-MINDEDNESS AND CHILD-RAISING TODAY

"I am 15 and I really want a baby. Should I have a baby?" This question, asked by a schoolgirl recently on Quora, the online crowd-sourced vehicle, provoked an avalanche of replies.

The unanimously negative comments thundered, "No, not now!", citing psychological and economic reasons and the detrimental practical impact on the baby, the family and the mother herself.

No one mentioned morality, religious belief or the distinction between married and unmarried cohabitation, nor did they refer to ethnicity or socio-economic conditions.

The answers reflect the cultural changes America has witnessed in recent decades as new values, attitudes and social practices have evolved. The institution of marriage is seen as diminished in value and status; morality gives way to self-interest; personal concerns displace longer social goals and—most disturbingly—a growing present-mindedness supplants long-term thinking. The ramifications are complex, with profound implications for many aspects of national life.

Our present-minded society is faced with problems that were foreseeable: unfunded governmental pension liabilities; deteriorating physical infrastructure; diminishing government-funded scientific research on which future innovation would be based; and short-sighted educational practices that do not provide the skills required for effective American performance in an internationally competitive world. That American high school students perform poorly relative to their peers in all other advanced nations is acknowledged, as is the fact that the rich U.S. today has the highest poverty rate, the largest income inequality and the greatest wealth inequality of any major economy in the world.

Rising social and economic inequality has become a national preoccupation, with class eclipsing race, gender, ethnicity, religion and geographic location as a factor in perceived well-being. Economists typically see class quantified in terms of income and wealth; sociologists focus on occupational status and education; anthropologists consider cultural awareness, values and attitudes. Real world experience, however, has shown "psychological orientations to the future" to be the key factor in class determination. Based on its degree of future-mindedness, each social class "exhibits behaviors that extend to all aspects of life: manners, consumption, child-rearing, politics or whatever" (Edward Banfield in The Unheavenly City).

Present-oriented people live moment-to-moment, lack self-control and are prone to improvidence and irresponsibility. Violence, sexual infidelity, drug addiction and criminality are more common among them. The future-minded are self-disciplined, plan ahead and persevere. Even with low income and limited schooling, the future-minded can be middle class and high-achieving in culture. Experience shows that a child's class culture is formed at home and in its earliest years, and the child's future-mindedness should be of general concern.

Compared to other advanced nations such as the Nordic countries, America is "lower class" in its thinking across the socioeconomic spectrum. To begin a national reconsideration we must start at the bottom.

We can give parents appropriate incentives, disincentives, support and encouragement to increase the future-mindedness of their children. We can encourage them to bring into the world children who are planned and wanted, who will be raised by their mature parents in stable family settings, and who are socialized from infancy to relate comfortably to others and to reflect self-respect and the self-confidence that will help them regard the future optimistically.

Praising a child's strengths more often than criticizing weaknesses pays big dividends. Encouragement and commendation of character traits such as perseverance, curiosity, courage, humor and kindness are reflected in a child's greater self-confidence, better relationships with others, better performance in school and in life.

Future-minded thinking is not a zero-sum game. It is better for the individual, better for the family, better for the community and better for society as a whole.

Financial capital, industrial capital and physical capital are important for a modern nation's well-being, but human capital—the personal attributes, aspirations, work ethic, knowledge and skills of the public—are even more so. Future-mindedness is a key aspect of human capital, and how to inculcate it is our greatest challenge.

August 2017

A HERO FOR TODAY

All healthy societies need role models and heroes – those we admire and respect, who reflect our standards of pride or shame, who inspire others to strive to achieve their full potential. Especially today, when national leaders of personal integrity, compassion and authenticity are in such short supply, we must celebrate those few we have.

Robert F. Smith, who electrified the audience at Morehouse College's recent Commencement exercises, is a prime candidate for our cheers. His surprise announcement of a personal gift to pay the entire college debt of the Morehouse graduating class's 396 students (estimated at some $20 million) was an outstanding moment in the history of U.S. philanthropy.

Stating clearly that he hoped to set an example, he challenged the Morehouse alumni present to play their part accordingly. "Let's make sure that every class has the same opportunity going forward, because we are enough to take care of our own community," he said. "We are enough to ensure we have all of the opportunities of the American Dream, and we will show it to each other through our actions and through our words and through our deeds!!"

Private philanthropy must be 'in addition to' NOT 'instead of' governmental programs. Its role is crucial in American life today.

With every HBCU (Historically Black College and University) in financial straits, Smith's message is important and timely. He is the richest black person in the United States, with a dazzling record of philanthropic gifts; but other black billionaires and multi-millionaires can follow his example by helping black students rise. "Intellectual capital has become the new currency of business and finance – and the promise of utilizing brainpower to move individuals, families, and even entire communities from poverty to prosperity within one generation has never been more possible than at this moment in time," Smith said in 2017 in an essay when he signed the Giving Pledge, joining Bill Gates, Warren Buffett and others in promising to contribute half their fortunes to charitable causes.

When Robert F. Smith's philanthropic activities are discussed in black churches, ministers would do well to cite the biblical commandment (Luke 10:37): "Go thou and do likewise."

June 2019

PERSONAL VIGNETTES

DR. MARTIN LUTHER KING, JR AND THE MARCH ON WASHINGTON

In the Spring of 1963, our friend Bayard Rustin asked my wife and me to join him for dinner with Martin Luther King Jr, whose formidable "Letter From Birmingham Jail" we had just read.

Bayard was working with A. Philip Randolph, head of the Sleeping Car Porters Union, to plan a mass rally in Washington, D.C. later that summer to focus national attention on black unemployment and to call for a public works program providing jobs for blacks. Although Randolph was the leader, Bayard handled the logistics and Dr. King was to be the chief speaker at the Lincoln Memorial on the 100th anniversary of Abraham Lincoln's signing of the Emancipation Proclamation.

They were asking friends for help in raising working capital, an effort which was going slowly because at first some major civil rights organizations, the NAACP and CORE among them, failed to support the event.

At the dinner, when I expressed fear that bringing together thousands of militant marchers could be counter-productive if they rioted, I was assured that the event would be serious in message but pacific in tone. My fear that hostile "Bull Connor-type" patrolmen might incite the marchers was answered with the reply that enough volunteer off-duty black policemen would be available to insure safety. And the President's office had told them that National Guard and U.S. Army forces would be available if necessary.

The spirit of Mahatma Gandhi and Henry David Thoreau was invoked; and Dr. King spoke so fervently that we were deeply moved. At the time, I was a salaried 33-year-old with three children and a pregnant wife; and a cup of coffee and a hot dog each cost a nickel.

When I wrote a pocket check for $1,000 to the Southern Christian Leadership Conference, Dr. King thanked us warmly. He noted that of all the major contributions he had ever received for the Southern Christian Leadership Conference, some 90% had come from Jews involved in the Civil Rights movement.

Soon after, the NAACP and other civil rights groups joined to support the March; 250,000 people attended; and Dr. King's "I Have a Dream" speech became part of American history.

The emotion generated by the 1963 March was a significant factor in the passage of the Civil Rights Act of 1964 and the Voting Act of 1965. And we are proud to have played even a modest role.

HEAF AND BLACK EDUCATION

In 1968, after years of serving on several Jewish philanthropic organizations (President, YM/YWHA of the Bronx; Trustee, active Board Member of the Federation of Jewish Philanthropies, etc.), I was delighted to be invited to join the Board of New York's Police Athletic League. In those days, PAL operated a number of recreational centers, but for the most part (like most youth organizations at the time) it was chiefly a bat-and-ball agency involved primarily in athletics and play streets.

I chose Harlem as my area of concern and hoped to focus on education. When, some years later, a new PAL facility opened in Harlem, I suggested creating an after school academic program for the center; and since neither funds nor staff were available, I offered to provide them. My fellow PAL Board member, Judge James "Skiz" Watson was an enthusiastic partner, and we moved ahead.

Although PAL eventually embarked on now widely celebrated educational activities, at the time we were out of phase with PAL's then-current thinking. The athletic staff running the new center felt that our academic workers would interfere with their athletic training programs; and Skiz and I agreed that we needed a separate entity and our own home. Mirian Acosta Sing, Principal of the Mott Hall School, and Fern Khan, Dean of Bank Street College, were early supporters whose help was invaluable.

A good friend, Gerald Freund, was happy to serve as our consultant. As a senior officer of the MacArthur Foundation, the Rockefeller Foundation and former Dean of Humanities of Hunter College, he seemed to know everyone and everything in the field; and he helped us build a staff and a program that seemed ideal.

The program was started as the 'Harlem Educational Activities Fund' (HEAF), and we moved to rented space in the renovated Hotel Theresa on 125th Street. All agreed that our challenge was not merely to perform what some others were doing but what they should be doing. HEAF was created as a trail blazing afterschool program which would produce inner city public school students who were ambitious, highly motivated and academically well-prepared to go on to high achievement. Future-mindedness and high aspirations; worthwhile long-term goals implemented by intense, self-disciplined efforts; self-confidence in one's ability to achieve and pride in such achievement—all were inculcated in our students, strongly, clearly and lovingly.

Three decades later, HEAF's track record is nationally acknowledged and celebrated—100% of our thousand-plus Harlem public school students graduate from high school and virtually all go on to four year colleges, with some 35% of our students entering graduate school (vs. 11% of all U.S. high school students). Our earliest students are now succeeding in impressive professional careers (one, a Lt. Colonel in the U.S. Army, others as doctors, teachers, scientists, etc.), and they are happy to serve as role models and mentors for those who follow.

Over the years, HEAF has been blessed with talented and dedicated Executive Directors, like Courtney Welsh, Danielle Moss Lee and Ruth Rathblott, devoted and expert professional staff and committed and enthusiastic Board Members. The results show what 'practical idealists' can achieve with encouragement and support. When HEAF-sponsored junior high school chess teams ranked Number One in the nation and when, with HEAF encouragement and financing, our chess instructor became the chess world's first black International Grand Master, I like to think that Gerry Freund (who died in 1997) and Skiz Watson (who died in 2001) looked down with pride on what we created together.

THE QUEEN OF WESTERN SAMOA AND THE CUB SCOUTS

Synergy — mutual re-inforcement or cooperative interaction — has always been a goal of mine in relating my various activities one to another. Writing articles which present the case for HEAF in the pages of The Harlem Times (DR, co-founder) or stimulating Yale alumni activity in programs of the Helping Africa Foundation (DR, Founding President) in Ghana are current examples.

An earlier instance took place in the 1960's, when my involvement with the Foreign Policy Association brought me to hear an afternoon talk by the Queen of Western Samoa.

She spoke enthusiastically about her support for the Samoan Boy Scout movement, and after her talk I asked her if she would like to visit an American Cub Scout meeting. She would be delighted, she said. I immediately called Sidney Offit, my friend and co-leader of Cub Scout Pack 606, to see if I could bring the Queen to a Cub Scout monthly meeting scheduled for that evening in the gymnasium of P.S. 6 on Madison Avenue and 81st Street. Sidney thought I was joking, of course, and expected me to bring some actress from Central Casting.

At 7:00PM, my wife and I escorted the exotically-gowned Queen to the second floor gymnasium of the darkened P.S. 6 school building.

When I stuck my head in the half-opened doorway to announce our presence, the excited, uniformed youngsters "fell in" in their assembled ranks; the bewildered expressions on the faces of the grownup leaders were memorable.

I introduced the Queen, who greeted the youngsters graciously, spoke warmly of scouting as an activity, and even sang them a Samoan song. The kids were blown away, my wife and I were delighted, and to this day my fellow Cub Scout leaders find it all hard to believe.

HOUSING FOR THE PERFORMING ARTS

How a failing residential development became a nationally-acclaimed "housing for the performing arts" project is recounted in Paul Goldberger's excellent New York Times article of August 2, 1976 (Page 28). The "back story" of how the financially –threatened Manhattan Plaza development was salvaged is more prosaic, but still bears telling.

The HRH Construction Company had planned a major middle income residential development to be financed under the New York State Mitchell-Lama program; and its president, Saul Horowitz Jr., chose Rose Associates, the company of his good friend, Fred Rose, as the project's renting and managing agent.

Planning on the project began in the boom year of 1974, but during construction New York underwent a steep recession and a softening real estate market. The state was able to finance only $65 million of the proposed $95 million mortgage, and construction stopped. Rose Associates faced the prospect of losing lucrative fees for providing services for the two 45 story towers containing 1600 apartments; so the HRH problem became ours as well.

The only project financing feasible at the time was the federal Section Eight low income housing program, which was proposed for the project by Roger Starr, New York's Housing and Development Administrator. Heated objections were raised by those who feared the destructive impact on midtown Manhattan by the introduction of large numbers of concentrated, dysfunctional poor.

At the time, I was engaged in Rose projects out of New York, but this was a company emergency that involved us all. I spent a day studying the site and the neighborhood and spoke with the vehement opposition; but the outlook seemed grim. It then occurred to me that Mike Todd, the theater and film producer, gave me our theme when he described his childhood family as "broke but not poor." By requiring our prospective low income Section Eight tenants also to be members of Actors Equity, the Musicians Union, Screen Actors Guild and the like, our tenants would be, like the Todds, middle class professionals without money.

When I suggested the concept to Roger Starr, he praised the creative thinking but asked, "Where in the Section Eight legislation does it refer to actors or musicians?" I replied, "Where does it forbid them?" After a long pause, Roger said, "Let's go for it. Bounce the idea off the Shuberts (New York's largest theater-owning group) and the Actors Equity people, and get a reaction from Clara Fox and her Settlement Housing Fund team."

At the Shubert meeting, Bernard Jacobs, the President, was opposed, but Gerald Schoenfeld, the Chairman, was open-minded. In time, he became a supporter and I referred objectors to him. After my many unanswered calls to Actors Equity, the president, Theodore Bikel, left word that since I was a real estate man and he hated real estate people, I should please stop bothering him. I asked Jerry Schoenfeld to work on Bikel, and he eventually got other actors to support us.

The Settlement Housing Fund was formally retained by Roger Starr to prepare a thorough study of the concept. Though Clara Fox was dubious at first, the Fund's eventual enthusiastic report—a 72-page blockbuster prepared by David Muchnick—convinced most remaining skeptics. Some local real estate owners fought the concept to the end, but they were overruled.

At Manhattan Plaza's formal opening in the Spring of 1977, the Mayor cut the ribbon, the 1,689 apartments were fully rented (70% to performing arts workers, 15% to elderly and handicapped, 15% to existing residents of the neighborhood); and within the first year the waiting list had over 3,000 names.

On July 13, 1977, nine million people in the New York area were affected by a power outage when lightning hit key electrical transmission lines. Looting and pillaging were widespread in public housing. In Manhattan Plaza, "broke-but-middle-class" tenants organized themselves: volunteers placed candles in stairwells and patrolled them; upper floor tenants were invited to spend the night on the living room couches of lower floor tenants. The entire Manhattan Plaza community was proud that no untoward incidents were reported, and the crisis created a sense of fellowship and camaraderie among neighbors.

My last involvement with Manhattan Plaza was to recruit the Rev. Rodney Kirk as Manager. Formerly on the staff of the Cathedral of St. John the Divine, he performed brilliantly for us, especially through his efforts when the AIDS epidemic hit New York.

Manhattan Plaza's success was applauded immediately, and the concept of 'housing for the performing arts' has since been widely implemented throughout the country.

BOSTON'S THRIVING WATERFRONT

A visitor today to Boston's vibrant Fort Point Channel area — with its museums, hotels, chic restaurants and artists' studios — might be surprised to learn that in 1967, when Kevin White was elected Boston's mayor, the area contained only decrepit warehouses and manufacturing lofts, all owned by the Boston Wharf Company. When our British real estate friends bought BWCo (90 buildings on 55 acres) they invited Rose Associates to supervise it for them, so its problems (and prospects) became ours.

The British had earlier invited Rose Associates to be their joint venture partners in the development of the State Street Bank building at 225 Franklin Street, Boston financial district's first post World War II office tower. David Rose, our leader, murmured, "Pioneers sometimes get scalped," and instead offered to be their partner in "Boston's second successful new office tower."

That opportunity presented itself when the British bought a site at Congress, High and Purchase Streets zoned for 400,000 sq. ft. of new construction and invited Rose Associates to join them. When I asked Hale Champion, Mayor White's chief planner (and a prominent advocate for good design), about the prospects for upzoning, he said, "We can do anything. Show us what you want to build and we will say yes or no."

The prominent architect Pietro Belluschi, Dean of M.I.T.'s School of Architecture, was Hale's design consultant, so I asked Belluschi what he would do with the site. He came up with a sketch for a handsome travertine and marble tower of 728,000 sq. ft. of rentable space.

My brother Fred and Uncle Dave were skeptical, but let me proceed with Belluschi. When the Boston Redevelopment Authority (BRA) announced their approval of plans for the 728,000 sq. ft. building I immediately called Fred and was greeted by a long pause. Finally, he said, "I guess I better call the team at Emery Roth to stop work on the 400,000 ft. building." Belluschi's handsome proposed building (with working drawings by Emery Roth) was soon rented to Keystone Custodian Funds. It became a "mortgage-out" and led the delighted British to ask me — and the excellent Rose Associates team I led — to supervise the renting of vacant loft space at the Boston Wharf Company, which they had recently purchased.

The Boston Wharf Company was founded in 1836 by a group of ship owners needing storage space to hold sugar and molasses for the city's sugar refineries. By 1930, the district was the center of the wool trade for much of the nation, but eventually the development of synthetic fibers led to the decline of New England's textile industry. Air freight and trucking displaced maritime shipping, and new uses had to be found for the handsome, well-preserved old loft and warehouse buildings.

In the 1970's, an artist studio building in Jamaica Plain burned down, and we invited the artists to consider space at Boston Wharf. The BRA scheduled public hearings on our controversial proposal to convert Boston Wharf lofts to residential and studio use, and the militant South Boston Irish community (known as Southies) — passionately opposed to gentrification, school integration and busing—turned out in large numbers to protest at the hearing. When I finished my testimony, the hearing officer sought questions, and the first speaker was an old man with a heavy brogue. "Mr. Rose," he said, "Can we assume that your proposed housing will be either subsidized or unsubsidized?" Warily, I replied, "Well that's one way of putting it." "Mr. Rose", he shouted, "if subsidized, you will bring us black muggers; if unsubsidized, fairy decorators. Mr. Rose, we don't want your black muggers or your fairy decorators in South Boston!" His supporters cheered, and the hearing was adjourned.

The next day the BRA ruled in our favor. The Jamaica Plain artists moved into our renovated structure on Farnsworth Street; and a vibrant arts community has thrived along Fort Point Channel ever since.

Our Boston story concludes with the development of One Financial Center, the 46 story, 1.3 million sq. ft. office tower directly across from South Station.

When, in the early 1980's, Mayor Kevin White casually inquired about our next major project, I thought immediately of the dramatic up-zoning of the Keystone Building's site, and I asked what he had in mind. He suggested I touch base with the BRA, whose staff had no current master plan but who referred me to urban planning sketches that Victor Gruen had prepared years before. The biggest future structure indicated was smack in the middle of the Dewey Square traffic center by South Station. When I naively asked who owned the site I was told that "There is no site; it is just where Victor Gruen thought Boston's biggest office tower should be." Owners of adjoining real estate could apply to purchase the city-owned land, and the BRA would happily redesign the awkward, anti-pedestrian Dewey Square.

The following week I asked Larry Bianchi, our friend and local real estate broker, to speak with the Boston Envelope Company, owners of a tumble-down loft facing Dewey Square. Pietro Belluschi, working with his local partner, (Yu Sing Jung of Jung Brannen) thought heroically and designed a handsome 46 story office tower on a one and a quarter acre site. The BRA loved his sketches, especially the dazzling 90 foot high glass-roofed atrium. Prospective tenants expressed interest and Chase Bank and Metropolitan Life Insurance Company were happy to explore financing. Bernie Strassner, our Chief Engineer, Morris Mansfield, our Chief Financial Officer, John Dineen, our Boston real estate attorney, Larry Bianchi, our real estate broker, and I performed our respective roles, and the rest is history.

PAT MOYNIHAN AND
FEDERAL HEALTH CARE

Daniel Patrick Moynihan, New York's great Senator, was a good friend; and from time to time we had lunch in New York at his favorite table at the Century Association. On one memorable occasion, he approached the table in a state of agitation, his jaw clenched, his face drained of color. I was afraid that he was about to have a stroke or a heart attack.

He had just been on a telephone call with Ira Magaziner, Hillary Clinton's deputy in preparing the Clinton administration's 1993 Health Security Act, unofficially nicknamed "Hillarycare."

As Chairman of the U.S. Senate committee responsible for the proposed legislation, Pat felt he had been frozen out of the investigations, confidential hearings and discussions prior to the bill's drafting. Now he was being asked to submit to his committee Magaziner's confidentially-prepared draft "without changing the dotting of an 'i' or the crossing of a 't'," Pat seethed.

"D.O.A. — Dead on Arrival," he raged, "Not a chance, not a prayer of its passing. And what breaks my heart is that Bob Dole (the Republican minority chair) and I had agreed on a more modest bill — not perfect, but one that could have been accepted!"

He pointed out that he and Dole had hoped to establish — for the first time ever — the federal government's involvement in health care. The legislation could be expanded and improved in due course. The crucial breakthrough had been possible, Pat felt, and now the opportunity would soon evaporate. "Legislation is like toilet training for a baby," said Pat. "If you miss your moment, you must wait for the right moment again. Who knows how many years will pass before the prospect of federal health legislation is again on the table?"

"Hillarycare" officially died on September 26, 1994. "Obamacare" was not approved until March 23, 2010.

BARACK OBAMA AND HAMLET'S MOTHER

As a contributor to his first Presidential campaign, I was invited to dinner with President Obama on his visit to New York during his first year in office.

He spoke briefly during cocktails and then sat for a while at each of several tables during dinner. On joining my table he asked for constructive suggestions we might have for him. I made clear I was an admirer, but suggested that he, as a law professor, was used to addressing sophisticated academic audiences. National political audiences require a different approach, I suggested, aimed more at those who 'feel' than those who 'think'. When Bill Clinton said, "I feel your pain," they felt he really cared.

I continued, "Your Harvard colleagues may feel you are pandering and that it is beneath you, but I suggest that when you speak more simply and evocatively to the public, you remember Hamlet's comment to his mother — "Assume a virtue if you have it not." When the evening ended and we said good night, President Obama shook my hand, looked me in the eye and said quietly, "Hamlet's mother!"

A short time later, the President was on television, speaking emotionally about his visit to a hurricane-damaged site. My wife commented, "He got your message."

THE TRIBAL CHIEF AND THE GOAT

The Yale Alumni Association, foreign real estate development and "witchcraft" (sorcery) would not normally be associated, but for me they came together in Ghana.

When I learned that Yale was seeking sponsorship for an African development conference to be held in Accra, Ghana and also that the son of a friend sought my involvement in a proposed real estate project in Ghana, I offered to sponsor the conference and to visit the real estate site.

The conference organizers asked if, as sponsor, I would like to attend and to speak, and I accepted both invitations for July 19, 2013. I spoke on "Development Challenges For Africa," which I saw as an interesting intellectual question.

The other conference participants spoke quietly to each other, while I boomed out loudly to the furthest person in the large tent. Furthermore, I had a printed text of my talk available for distribution to the press. By the next day, I became "known" in Ghana.

One thing led to another. My friend John Whitehead, formerly of Goldman Sachs and the State Department, was involved in African charities, and he asked for a donation to bring fresh, safe drinking water to thousands of Ashanti tribe members who did not have it. Another tribe sought help with street lighting at a dangerous and dark traffic intersection. I met the President of Ghana, whose wife was particularly interested in helping elderly, abandoned widows who had been proclaimed "witches" by those seeking to seize the property of the dead husbands. And the W.E.B. DuBois Memorial Center in Accra, containing DuBois' own library, his personal papers and his burial site, was in a state of total deterioration.

In due course, these conditions led to my creating the Helping Africa Foundation. My designation as the Ashanti King's "Honorary Grandson" and my "enstoolment" as a tribal chieftain followed. At my installation, in full tribal regalia, I found myself holding a live goat on a rope. When I asked what to do with the goat I was told, "You could donate it to the poor," which, of course, I was happy to do.

The tribal leaders were kind enough to send me the "stool" and my full tribal regalia, which I am ready to wear on any appropriate occasion.

PENTAGON CITY: THE URBAN VILLAGE

Pentagon City, in Arlington, Virginia, is today a nationally-celebrated, vibrant mini-city whose Metro Station is one of the busiest in the Washington system.

In 1977, New York-based Rose Associates was invited by the Cafritz-Tompkins partnership to implement their long-envisioned "urban village" just south of the Pentagon. Prominent developers Morris Cafritz and Charles H. Tompkins had the foresight to acquire 190 acres of strategically-located farm land in 1946 for $1,500,000. Tompkins died in 1956, Cafritz in 1964, before the site was ripe for its full potential. Some 100 acres of the assemblage had been sold off for development of modest warehouses and commercial structures, but the key 85 acres surrounding the planned Metro Station were retained.

When the Metro Station was to open, Cafritz president Martin Atlas turned to New York-based Rose Associates to establish a "sense of place" around the station at 12th and South Hayes Streets, just south of Route I-395 and Army-Navy Drive.

Initial studies showed that a major retail center, headquarters office buildings, high rise rental and condominium residences and a major hotel were indicated; and I invited our friend, Melvin Simon, the nation's prime retail center developer, to join the team to develop the mall.

The high-density zoning we sought was strenuously challenged by nearby residents who opposed the additional traffic they expected the complex to generate. The Virginia Supreme Court definitively turned down the hostile appeals, and the Fashion Centre at Pentagon City (also known as the Pentagon City Mall) opened on October 5, 1989. The 170 retailers and restaurants, the Ritz Carlton Pentagon City Hotel and the stunning Nordstrom's and Macy's department stores drew raves.

In the mad crush of opening day ceremonies, I ran into my nemesis, the lady who for years had led the opposition to our plans. After having had to wait to enter the sparkling Nordstrom's department store, she complained to me that it was not large enough.

I was silent for a moment, restrained myself and then replied quietly, "Next time we will try to do better."

LINCOLN CENTER

For over six decades, I have followed New York's public controversies on cultural, economic and political questions and occasionally I have written or spoken publicly about them. Sometimes applauded, sometimes attacked, I assure you it is more fun to be cheered than jeered. An instance of each involved the planning of Lincoln Center and the redevelopment of Times Square.

On April 20, 1958, the New School for Social Research hosted a discussion of the proposed cultural conglomeration to be called Lincoln Center. The three-person panel consisted of a representative of the New York City Planning Commission to explain the details; Jane Jacobs, the militant activist opposed to large-scale development; and a spokesman for the Real Estate Board of New York to defend the concept.

At the last minute, the Real Estate Board speaker fell ill, and they desperately sought an emergency replacement. So it was that I found myself facing a Greenwich Village audience of several hundred militant supporters of Jane Jacobs. Her opposition to insensitive large-scale city planning made her a local celebrity, and her troops rallied.

The city planner spoke first, presenting slides of the neighborhood and maps and sketches of the large cultural center that was proposed.

Jane Jacobs spoke next, launching a savage attack on all aspects of the proposal, including an emotional account of the present community life that would be destroyed. Her major themes were: A) the area being demolished (like her beloved Greenwich Village) had diversity, character, human scale, "eyes-on-the-street," etc., while the proposed "towers in a park" were sterile, lifeless and uninviting, without the amenities that made cities livable; B) existing street and traffic patterns would be destroyed, with adverse effects on neighboring areas; and C) the concept of bringing together opera, symphony, ballet and similar components made no sense whatsoever because no one went directly from one to another. She expressed her contempt for sterile master-planned efforts like New York's Stuyvesant Town and St. Louis' Pruitt-Igoe and praised unplanned areas that throbbed with life. To summarize, she boomed out, "The vast bungle called Lincoln Center is devastatingly unjust."

Running out of time, she hastily made her final point as if revealing a scandalous secret: that underlying the whole project was a fraud, a giant scam. The multi-millionaire Joseph Kennedy family, having acquired much of the area's property at bargain prices, now sought to unload their assemblage at inflated values and make a killing, at the public's expense! The audience roared wildly.

When they calmed down, she continued, "Our final speaker, this nice young man representing the Real Estate Board, may be too naive to understand the scam—unless, of course, HE IS PARTY TO IT!" With that, she gestured to me; and I was greeted with boos, jeers and shouts of "fraud" and "scam" as I began to speak.

Slowly, clearly, loudly, I acknowledged the importance of her first points (ignoring the charge of fraud) but maintained that fair-minded observers had considered and dismissed them. Each of the components that would occupy the site—opera, ballet, theater—needed an expensive new structure; and fundraising would be enhanced by a joint effort. Adam Smith's "invisible hand" would supply the supporting amenities, such as restaurants and hotels, once the economic demand was clear. Relocation services and assistance would be provided to those being displaced. More importantly, a dramatic new public space would be created for New York—a tourist destination, an entertainment center for students and visitors, and a new iconographic image for New York, the world's most exciting city.

Ignoring the continuing catcalls, I resolutely made my case, finishing to a smattering of polite applause along with derisive shouts and jeers.

Jane Jacobs carried the day. The critic Lewis Mumford was in the audience, and on the basis of her attack he helped her get financing for the book she wanted to write, "The Death and Life of Great American Cities," which became the bible for anyone opposing large scale city planning.

Jane Jacobs' fears for the displaced residents proved justified. Robert Moses' promised relocation assistance never materialized for the 7,000 displaced poor minority families, and few of the 4,400 new housing units were for them. The human misery and hardship that followed was profound.

The moral? Future city planning efforts require both the Moses and Jacobs insights. We must consider human needs and concerns along with desirable brick-and-mortar physical development.

Lincoln Center today is a civic triumph, but I shall always remember April 20, 1958 with chagrin.

TIMES SQUARE

I first became involved with the city planning aspects of Times Square in 1981, when Brendan Gill asked me to join a newly-formed group called The Committee to Reclaim Times Square. Brendan had led the Municipal Art Society's successful campaign to save Grand Central Station from the unhappy fate of Penn Station; and he had led the efforts to preserve the Jefferson Market Courthouse on Sixth Avenue and 10th Street. Now he was concerned that misguided efforts to re-plan Times Square would be counter-productive.

By 1980, Times Square was a run-down travesty of its former glory as the center of New York cultural life. 42nd Street, which once had 35 theaters, then had only ten, chiefly cinemas, some of them pornographic. Formerly known as the "crossroads of the world," the area had become an urban wasteland, with drug dealing, prostitution, seedy hotels and massage parlors, and with former elegant restaurants and chic boutiques replaced by fast food outlets and porn shops. Planners were speaking of four massive office towers to be built at 42nd Street and Broadway and Seventh Avenue. Brendan feared that the once-vibrant street life would be replaced with ground floor sterility like that of the office towers on Sixth Avenue.

Although I shared his street level concern, I agreed with the rationale behind the office towers, so I could not join his group. We kept in touch throughout the planning and implementation process, however, and worked together to insure that the area kept its identity as an entertainment magnet, both for tourists and New Yorkers.

At a key session of a Planning Commission advisory committee on which we both served, I spoke enthusiastically of the mega signs that were proposed for the planned office buildings, and Brendan beamed his approval. He did, however, express disdain for the emerging aesthetic; and shortly before his death he wrote, "The culture of the country as a whole is rapidly becoming Disneyfied, and the practice of architecture is bound to reflect it."

Times Square today does not bear out Brendan's fear that it would be "flooded with white collar workers who go home at 5PM." The area did not become bland and corporate, but neither did it keep the raunchy, Damon Runyonesque flavor that he loved. Brendan would probably have deplored the crowded pedestrian mall, current traffic patterns and the fact that tourists posing for photos with costumed cartoon characters have largely displaced the city's natives.

The signage and lights we fought for are world famous and have achieved their goal of creating a festive atmosphere for the area. About all the rest, opinions vary.

ADOLF EICHMANN IN JERUSALEM

In May 1960 the world learned that Adolf Eichmann, the Nazi fugitive who had been a major villain in the Holocaust—the annihilation of millions of Jews—had been captured in Argentina by Israeli agents and transported to Israel.

David Ben Gurion, Israel's Prime Minister, was determined to bring Eichmann to trial in a showcase proceeding that would present to the world the detailed story of the Nazi proposed "Final Solution," their plan for the total elimination of world Jewry.

Gideon Hausner, Israel's Attorney General and Eichmann's chief prosecutor, and Moshe Landau, one of the trial's three presiding judges, were friends of my uncle, David Rose. As a result, several family members—I among them—were invited to attend some of the trial sessions.

Hannah Arendt, the prominent political theorist, reported on the trial for The New Yorker magazine in what became a widely-discussed book, "Eichmann in Jerusalem: A Report on the Banality of Evil." My reflections on the trial differed dramatically from hers.

Arendt, a German Jewish intellectual and a one-time mistress of the prominent German philosopher and Nazi apologist Martin Heidegger, wrote of the pettiness, insensitivity—in short, the banality—of this limited, spiritually numb murderer of millions, who suffered no remorse whatsoever because, he maintained, he was only acting under orders.

In the crowded, attentive courtroom, I thought little about the drab little man in the "glass box"; but I found myself pondering the question of vicious anti-Semitism—the longest, most intense, multi-faceted ethno/religious hatred in history.

Then, and ever since, I came to agree with Jean-Paul Sartre, Barbara Tuchman and others that "anti-Semitism is independent of its object," that it reflects the psychological needs and weaknesses of the anti-Semite, that it is an exercise in scapegoating others for the misfortunes of the anti-Semite, who is unable to understand the actual sources of his difficulties and seeks someone to blame.

Writing in 1945, Sartre portrayed U.S. anti-black racism as "the anti-Semitism of the new world." He described the typical anti-Semite as a lower middle class white collar proletarian fearfully and resentfully threatened by social change for which he was unprepared and against which he could not compete.

The questions I wrestled with at the Eichmann trial have again become relevant with the emergence of the Alt-Right in America and the resurgence of worldwide anti-Semitism (except in China, where the public is philo-Semitic!).

Sartre's answer was that Jews should be their "authentic best selves," not wallow in self-pity or feelings of victimization but aspire to the highest levels of achievement. That strikes me as still the best and most productive response we can make.

The vicious anti-Semitic rantings of Louis Farrakhan in America today and the failure of prominent black leadership figures to refute him pose a continuing quandary. With anti-Semitic feelings dramatically higher among blacks than among Americans generally, the natural alliances for civil rights and civil justice are weakened; and everyone loses. Given the historic support by Jews of black causes, this is particularly sad.

There are those who believe that scapegoats will always be sought by failures and paranoids, and that, in varying degrees and in varying situations, Jews will always be vulnerable. We can only pray that it is not so.

DEBATING THE MULLAHS

At a conference in Doha, Qatar in early 2004 (sponsored by the Brookings Institution and the Emir of Qatar), I found myself on a panel with a prominent conservative Iman, discussing the possible exposure of madrassah students to secular education in addition to, not instead of, their current religious fare. Liberal young Muslims in the audience applauded and an Al-Jazeera representative invited me to continue the discussion for them the next day, to present the Western view of the goal of a humanistic education. Again, young Muslims applauded and an Iranian journalist asked for my business card.

Back in New York, I was surprised, but pleased, to be invited to participate by telephone in an English language political discussion the following week on Teheran TV. The broadcast was scheduled for 4:00 PM New York time (11:00 PM Teheran time) and the subject was the 25th anniversary of the Muslim revolution in Iran.

When I told my wife I had accepted, she asked, "What do you know about the Iranian revolution?" I replied, "Joanna, I have a week to learn!" That broadcast set the pattern for my monthly presentations on Iranian TV for the next two years.

Topics for discussion ranged from the role of Sunnis and Kurds in Iraqi politics to the impact on the U.S. economy of OPEC price rises, from an Arab League Summit Conference in Tunisia to the U.N.'s resolutions on Israel's activities in Gaza. In each case, I had a week to learn the views of informed American liberals and to prepare my comments. When I was hopelessly out of my depth (e.g. on AIDS

113

at an HIV conference in Bangkok), I suggested other speakers—authorities from the Brookings Institution, the Council on Foreign Relations, etc. Other American participants on the program from time to time ranged from Noam Chomsky on the the Left to David Malpass (now Donald Trump's Under Secretary for International Affairs in the Treasury) on the Right.

I enjoyed the challenge of these sessions and tried hard to present – tactfully but clearly – what I understood to be the American position. This continued for two years, until my final discussion on the Iranian nuclear program. On that session, the Vice President of Iran gave an impassioned defense of Iran's nuclear aspirations. I got carried away and was not properly respectful in demolishing his weak arguments.

That was my last invitation to speak on Iranian TV. I miss the challenge of presenting America's views to a hostile foreign audience, but I was pleased to learn later that State Department monitors of the broadcasts felt I had been an effective spokesman.

HORACE MANN AND TILLY

The Horace Mann School for Boys, whose predecessor institution was founded in 1887 by Columbia's Nicholas Murray Butler as a teachers training school, had evolved by the 1930's into New York's outstanding private secondary school.

Its imposing campus and facilities on West 246th Street in the Riverdale section of the Bronx were presided over by the formidable Dr. Charles C. Tillinghast, a respected figure in secondary education (he was a Trustee of Brown University, among other roles), who led an excellent faculty proud of preparing students for admission to the nation's finest colleges.

When my parents learned that friends in Mt. Vernon, NY, where I grew up, sent their sons there in preference to the local public high school, they made inquiries and were impressed by what they learned. In due course, my brothers Fred (H.M. '40), Elihu (H.M. '50), and I (H.M. '47) all attended.

The Horace Mann I entered in 1941 as a First Former (7th grader) was a revelation. The students wore jackets and neckties and (as I recall, my first) long trousers, addressed grownups as "yes, sir" and "no, ma'am," and looked forward to attending Ivy League colleges. The excellent library, with imaginative displays and varied student committees and activities, was the heart of the school; and the range of student publications, clubs and extra-curricular activities was stimulating. The atmosphere was literate, thoughtful and moral, of students being prepared for productive and fulfilling lives.

Most talk of secondary schooling today focuses on test preparation and S.A.T. scores. In the Horace Mann of the 1940's the dedicated faculty encouraged intellectual curiosity and love of their subjects. English teachers like Alfred Baruth and William Blake, teachers of chemistry like Harry Williams or of physics like Robert Payne, language teachers like William Nagle or Ernest Dodge and others, taught at college level, inspiring in their students high aspirations and a love of life-long learning.

Prominent alumni provided role models, but the most powerful message was sent by the Headmaster, Charles Tillinghast, in his personal involvement in school affairs and by his weekly talks in what was called Chapel. Tilly (as everyone referred to him) was a memorable figure of my childhood. His magisterial demeanor, his stentorian voice and his authoritative manner made me feel I was in the presence of a biblical prophet.

He exuded a sense of propriety—there were things that were done and not done. Not priggishness, but ethical conduct, not fervor, but "doing the right thing" was expected. Unlike the other academics, intellectuals and religious leaders with whom I was familiar, I did not associate Tilly with wit, sarcasm, hyperbole or even with humor. He embodied earnestness and probity. Tilly belonged to a different age; and in a day when so few figures in public life evoke our respect, I confess I miss his type.

In later years, when I became a member of the H.M. Board of Trustees and eventually the Board Chairman, I wondered about how Tilly would have regarded the school's evolution that changing times demanded. (When I proposed H.M.'s merger with the adjoining Barnard School, one cynic commented, "all developers try to enlarge the plot." When we moved to go co-ed, our constituency approved enthusiastically.)

In retrospect, Horace Mann alumni of my vintage feel we were privileged to have benefitted from a remarkable educational experience. On balance, I am sure that Tilly would have been proud to learn that in 2018, rating agencies still note Horace Mann as the best private school in New York.

AMERICAN EXCEPTIONALISM AT ITS BEST

The Marshall Plan—America's unprecedented multi-billion dollar post-World War II program to rebuild a devastated Europe—was the only instance in the history of Western Civilization when, after a catastrophic war, the victor asked the vanquished, "How can we help?"

Similar in spirit to the Marshall Plan was the United States program to rebuild the destroyed economies of Central and Eastern Europe after the Fall of the Berlin Wall in 1989 and demise of Stalinist communism, the dissolution of the USSR and the end of the Cold War.

Known officially as the SEED Act (Support for Eastern European Democracy), the program introduced by President George H.W. Bush created Enterprise Funds to help restore free-market economies in nations previously dominated by the Soviet Union. A dozen separate Enterprise Funds were eventually established, one each for Poland, Hungary, etc. Each had an independent, highly-qualified Board of Directors whose members—drawn from the private sector—had experience in investments, banking and economics. A unique combination of public funding, private loans and equity investments enabled these Funds to achieve remarkable results. Companies, jobs and a home mortgage industry were created; investment professionals were trained; women were employed and vibrant free-market influences resounded throughout formerly government-controlled economies.

The Baltic American Enterprise Fund—to be active in Latvia,

Lithuania and Estonia—was announced by President Bill Clinton in 1994, and I was privileged to be named Vice Chairman. The Chairman, Ambassador Roz Ridgway, my fellow Directors—Kim Davis, Paul Elicker, Hughlyn Fierce, Juris Padegs—and I plunged into what became an exhilarating and profoundly satisfying experience for us all. Our quarterly Board meetings were stimulating, and our annual Board trips to the Baltics were among the highlights of my year.

I led a search committee to select a President and CEO, and we happily settled on Brewster Campbell, a retired Bank of America executive with extensive international experience. Our General Counsel, Robert Odle, rounded out a team that performed wonders. After Bruce Campbell retired, Richard Sheridan, a longtime Fund senior executive who had performed splendidly in our banking and finance arrangements, was elected President.

Formally established in July, 1994 with a mandated 15-year life, the Baltic American Enterprise Fund (BalAEF) was granted $50 million in U.S. Funds to lend or invest in Baltic activities. By 2008, at our formal close, the Fund had provided 19,813 loans to home owners and had raised over $270 million in external funding. Over its lifetime, BalAEF lent or invested $794 million to support more than 125 businesses engaged in tourism, light manufacturing, food processing, wood handling, transportation and warehousing. At its inception, the Fund's home mortgage program was the only one of its kind, and it claimed 100% of the market. Within a year, local banks throughout the Baltics followed suit, with lending products modeled after ours. Within five years, our mortgage operation was but a fraction of the market. The Baltic American Enterprise Fund had spearheaded the creation of a residential financing industry.

BalAEF eventually returned to the U.S. government $25 million, and with universal approval passed on to its "legacy"—the Baltic-American Freedom Foundation—an endowment of over $35 million. Led by Kim Davis as Chairman and with a new Board of Directors, the Foundation, created in 2010, provides a range of internships for university students and recent graduates from the three countries, academic research activities and a Leadership Academy for high school students. In addition, the Foundation has granted millions in a variety of scholarships.

Yes, at its best America can be "exceptional," and we should encourage our government to keep it so.

EAST HAMPTON—
A FIFTY YEAR LOVE AFFAIR

My wife and I first visited East Hampton in the Spring of 1964 as weekend guests of Ben and Judy Heller at their home on Jericho Lane. We loved what we saw, and that same weekend we rented the Lily Pond Lane home of Mrs. Harry Dorsey Watts for the approaching summer.

Jim Amaden, the leading local broker, walked us through Joseph Greenleaf Thorpe's shingle style 1905 gem, and we were charmed. "We'll take it," Joanna cried. As a real estate professional, I replied that you cannot commit yourself until you consider all other homes available. Jim showed us another half-dozen prospects, and at the end we committed to rent the house on Lily Pond Lane for the Summer of 1964.

The first season was a roaring success. Our four children, then ranging in age from one to seven, loved splashing in the surf and digging in the sand on Main Beach, taking pony rides at Stony Hill Stables, visiting the Penny Candy Shop in Water Mill, feeding the ducks at the Nature Trail pond and searching stealthily for wild animals in the underbrush. They found friends in the summer programs at Guild Hall, the East Hampton Library and the Jewish Center of the Hamptons. Picking strawberries was a treat for these city children, and the kite-flying and sand castle contests on Main Beach were exciting challenges.

Grownup family members and visiting friends enjoyed golf and tennis, deep-sea fishing off Montauk and side trips to the Whaling Museum in Sag Harbor, nature sites on Shelter Island or the Quonset hut of the Museum of Antique Automobiles in Southampton (which proudly displayed a 1933 Pierce Arrow owned by Al Capone!)

Everyone loved the massive Fourth of July fireworks at Main Beach, the bustling LVIS summer fair and the endless clambakes, barbeques and charity fund-raising events.

As major art collectors and he as dealer, the Hellers were key members of the East Hampton art community, and they introduced us to friends and acquaintances who added sparkle to summer gatherings. Jackson Pollock, Willem de Kooning, Ibram Lassaw, Norman Bluhm, Balcomb Greene, Alfonso Ossorio, Claus and Helen Hoie, Warren Brandt, Bill King, Sheridan Lord, Jane Freilicher, Robert Dash and dealer Andre Emmerich were prominent at parties, along with architects Richard Meier, Peter Blake and Norman Jaffe. At one of Miriam (Mimi) Schapiro and Paul Brach's occasional poker games, I recall losing a modest amount to the widow of novelist James Jones; and literary critic Dwight Macdonald once shocked our children by swimming nude in our pool.

The outstanding characteristic of the community was its human scale. The small mom-and-pop stores on Main Street and Newtown Lane; the all-you-can-eat fundraising breakfasts of the Veterans of Foreign Wars at the American Legion Hall, at which men cooked and their wives cleaned up; the Memorial Day Parade (where it seemed that more of the town paraded than watched); the Clothesline Art Sale at Guild Hall (at which neighbors bought their friends' work); the clambakes run by volunteers at the Amagansett Fire House; the celebrated chefs Pierre Franey and Jacques Pepin cooking their specialties at the Springs Fair — all were projects by neighbors for neighbors. The audience capacity at the Old Post Office cinema on Newtown Lane was so small that the experience seemed intimate, and at Guild Hall, the summer theater, many in the audience knew the actors and interns, who often were staying in their homes. East Hampton exuded a feeling of community in the best sense of the word.

As each Labor Day approached, we gave Jim Amaden a list of suggested repairs and improvements, and they were always finished before Memorial Day began another memorable summer. After six years of this, Mrs. Watts sent word that, in effect, she was tired of being our caretaker and that we should purchase the property and take care of it ourselves. We did, and one wonderful summer followed another. Today, our children and grandchildren share our feelings about this idyllic setting.

The faces of yesterday are gone, but the rhythms of life continue; and the magical air, light and lushness of East Hampton remain.

'CHICKEN LITTLE'
AND ECONOMIC FORECASTING

When I was asked to speak on our economy at the April 4, 2008 national conference of the Yale Alumni Real Estate Association, I prepared by reviewing all the relevant data I could find, and the conflicting signals were bewildering.

On March 14, 2008 I heard President Bush tell the Economic Club of New York (who cheered) how strong and resilient the American economy was; and as he was speaking, Bear Stearns announced it was seeking Chapter 11 bankruptcy protection. Federal Reserve Chairman Ben Bernanke told Congress he expected the economy to grow in the second half of 2008 and to be solid in 2009, while the Consumer Confidence Survey showed public confidence (historically an accurate predictor) had declined to its lowest level in 16 years, and the Conference Board's index of leading indicators fell for the fifth consecutive month. Goldman Sachs proclaimed that home prices in California were over-valued by 40%; and my mentor, Yale's Nobel Laureate professor Robert J. Shiller (author of Irrational Exuberance) predicted that home prices could be in gradual decline for five years or more.

Low quality/high risk housing loans based on weak underwriting standards were a national fact of life; and opaque and unregulated financial instruments, like credit default swaps (CDS), which distributed worthless mortgage-backed securities, went largely unexamined.

I tried to present my worrisome conclusions in a thought-provoking, but entertaining manner, and the talk was well-received. In the audience was the editor of The Wharton Journal, who praised my presentation, but found it too pessimistic. On the spot he commissioned me to write an article for The Wharton Journal Fall 2008 issue, convinced that by then my views would be more upbeat.

During August, 2008 I once again applied due diligence in my preparation, and once again I was frightened by what I found. Public talks by government officials were optimistic, but U.S. consumer confidence was its lowest level in 30 years and an estimated 10 million U.S. families had negative equity (value lower than debt) in their homes. Auto loans and credit card defaults were soaring and bank failures were increasing. The Federal Deposit Insurance Corp. was at its most over-extended position since its creation in 1933.

When I submitted my piece, the Editor (who felt that the worst of the recent economic decline was behind us and that the recovery had started) laughingly compared me to Chicken Little, convinced that the sky was falling.

The Wharton Journal Fall 2008 issue was published on September 1st. On September 11th I received a gracious complimentary letter from Paul Volcker (former Federal Reserve Chairman) and on September 15th Lehman Brothers filed for Chapter 11 bankruptcy, the largest financial failure in U.S. history. On September 29, 2008, the Dow Jones Industrial Average fell 777 points, the second largest drop in history.

The moral? Economic forecasting is more art than science. Given the complex interaction of 'knowns' and 'unknowns' – economic and psychological, political and social, national and international, we must be prepared for surprises. In spite of politically-inspired nonsense to the contrary, prudence should dictate caution when major flashing yellow warning signals warn of trouble

ADDENDA

STILL FOCUSED ON THE FUTURE, IN WORD AND DEED

Nonagenarian Daniel Rose lives out the tikkun olam ethic.

Daniel Rose is a prominent real estate developer and philanthropist, widely known for his award-winning essays and speeches on a wide range of topics, from economics to racial relations. He also has much to say about American Jewry and its future.

Contrary to most observers these days, he's an optimist.

While sociologists and religious leaders worry about the growing number of Jewish youth who are unaffiliated and disengaged from communal and religious life, Rose points to the fact that 94 percent of respondents in the 2013 Pew survey of American Jews say they are proud to be Jewish.

"I look forward while most others look backward," Rose, 89 and still working full-time, told me over the course of several lengthy conversations at his midtown office.

His insights on why and how Jewish life will flourish, and his deep involvement with the black community, offer the unique perspective of someone whose words and actions have had a lasting impact on our society over many decades.

Assessing Jewish life in America today, Rose, who describes himself as a deeply involved cultural Jew, said that assimilation and intermarriage are realities that can be lamented but not undone. "The future of a healthy, vibrant and sustainable Jewish community in

America calls for the acknowledgment of a broad spectrum of beliefs and the ability to deal with each other respectfully," he said.

Rose insists that American Judaism can flourish if it is open to everyone, and promotes the kind of "life-enhancing values" like tzedakah, tikkun olam and the recognition of the dignity of each life, that are at the core of our heritage.

"We must reach out to the spouses and children of intermarriages, make them feel welcome and encourage them to embrace the Jewish ethos," he said, not for theological reasons but "for their own self-respect and benefit because it offers the life-affirming incentives of curiosity, endless questioning and great intellectual ferment." Only Judaism, Rose says, "believes the world was not created perfect, but rather that it is up to each of us to improve it."

The key is not that Jews are a Chosen People, but that "we can feel part of a Choosing People with a moral obligation to be a producer rather than a consumer — to leave our bit of the world a little better than what we found."

In his professional role with Rose Associates, a New York-based real estate corporation that he chairs, he led the development of Pentagon City in Alexandria, Va., and One Financial Center in Boston. But his great passions are philanthropy and writing essays and speeches. He won the Cicero Speechwriting Award on six different occasions, and Kirkus Reviews named a collection of his essays and speeches, "Making a Living, Making a Life," as one of the Best Books of 2015.

That collection includes a number of topics of particular interest to Jewish readers, ranging from Rose's role as a guest on Iranian national television for two years as a "defender of American values," to the qualities and values of tzedakah, to his personal views on Judaism. He says he would accept into the faith anyone who identifies as a Jew because most important is choosing to be part of the community rather than basing identity on one's bloodline.

Rose is proud of his own family history. He spoke of one great-grandfather, Simon Jacob Rose (1820-1905), an entrepreneurial type who left Poland, grew etrogim for a time, built houses in Jerusalem and eventually came to America in 1870. He settled in New York City, bought and sold properties, and always had strong ties to Israel and Jewish social, educational and cultural causes.

Rose's other great-grandfather, Menachem Rubinstein, was a quiet Jerusalem scholar so pious that the chief rabbi of Jerusalem referred to him as a lamed vavnik, one of the 36 righteous people in each generation on whose merit the world survives, according to legend.

Rose attended Yale in the class of 1951 and is proud that each of his four children went to Yale.

The Rose family has long been associated with Jewish communal life. Daniel's brothers, Frederick and Elihu, played leadership roles in Jewish organizations, including UJA-Federation of New York, the 92nd Street Y and the Technion in Israel. Daniel was president of the Jewish Community Centers of America, the National Jewish Welfare Board, and the YM/YWHA of the Bronx, was on the board of the Jewish Publication Society and a founding member of Technion's New York partnership with Cornell University, Cornell Tech, whose new campus is on Roosevelt Island.

Regarding Israel, Rose said his family was close to and supportive of founding Prime Minister David Ben-Gurion, Prime Minister Golda Meir and other leaders. But he said the decision to allow the Orthodox chief rabbinate to marginalize non-Orthodox rabbis "made my parents' generation sad, makes my generation angry — and doesn't matter at all to millennials because they don't think of Israel's problems as their problems."

That's one reason why Rose asserts that the degree of engagement with the non-Jewish spouses and children of Jews today will determine the future of American Jewry.

'The Right Thing To Do'

In the spring of 1963, Rose, through his close friend, civil rights leader Bayard Rustin, met personally with Rev. Martin Luther King Jr., who was seeking support for the planned March on Washington to promote civil and economic rights for black Americans. When

Rose made a major donation, King thanked him and noted that 90 percent of the most significant gifts for the cause came from the Jewish community. The march that August attracted huge crowds and is best remembered for King's "I have a dream" speech.

Since then Rose has been deeply involved in promoting racial equality "because," he said, "it's the right thing to do."

He is a founder of and remains chair of the Helping Africa Foundation, a New York-based charity that seeks to improve "health, education and social welfare conditions in Sub Sahara Africa," according to its website. He takes particular pride in having helped to create and sustain the Harlem Educational Activities Fund (HEAF), a trail-blazing after-school program encouraging youngsters in Harlem to achieve academic excellence. The emphasis is on "future-mindedness and high aspirations," Rose said, and promoting "self-discipline and self-confidence" in students. "Always think ahead," Rose says. "Failing to prepare is preparing to fail."

The program, marking its 30th anniversary this year, is cited nationally for its successes, with 100 percent of the thousand-plus Harlem public school students graduating from high school. Almost all go on to a four-year college; 35 percent enter graduate school (compared to the national average of 11 percent). Rose stays in touch with alumni who have gone on to impressive careers as doctors, teachers and scientists.

He believes in the uniqueness, magnitude and importance of American philanthropy. In a speech he gave at the Oxford Literary Festival at Christ Church College three years ago, he noted that private philanthropy tends to be innovative and creative, and that it is "more entrepreneurial, more cost-effective and more swiftly responsive to public needs than government," especially in areas like "culture, education and scientific research."

He asserted: "All who can afford to do so should follow their charitable intent, answering the biblical question:'Am I my brother's keeper?' with the reply: 'Yes, I am.'"

Through his philanthropic efforts, from supporting Israel and

Jewish causes to giving hope and opportunity to youngsters in Harlem, Dan Rose has spent a lifetime on that path of caring for others.

Gary Rosenblatt
Jewish Week
August 20, 2019

DANIEL ROSE PRESENTED WITH THE ALBERT NELSON MARQUIS LIFETIME ACHIEVEMENT AWARD BY MARQUIS WHO'S WHO®

Marquis Who's Who, the world's premier publisher of biographical profiles, is proud to present Daniel Rose with the Albert Nelson Marquis Lifetime Achievement Award. An accomplished listee, Mr. Rose celebrates many years' experience in his professional network, and has been noted for achievements, leadership qualities, and the credentials and successes he has accrued in his field. As in all Marquis Who's Who biographical volumes, individuals profiled are selected on the basis of current reference value. Factors such as position, noteworthy accomplishments, visibility, and prominence in a field are all taken into account during the selection process.

A seasoned professional with more than five decades of experience in his industry, Mr. Rose is a leader in real estate and urban development. He has studied at Yale University and Sorbonne University in Paris, and he has multiple honorary doctorates from the Technion - Israel Institute of Technology, Long Island University, and the New York University Tandon School of Engineering. Mr. Rose's expertise in urban development has afforded him a successful career throughout which he has held positions such as chairman, president, and chief executive officer of Rose Associates, Inc., and other organizations. His most notable professional endeavors include the development of Pentagon City in Washington, DC, and many office buildings in Boston,

MA, including the One Financial Center office tower. As a consultant, he created the concept of housing for the performing arts for New York's Manhattan Plaza complex.

A leader in his local community as well, Mr. Rose is active civically, having previously served with the U.S. Air Force as an intelligence analyst and Russian language specialist during the Korean War. He has sat and continues to sit on several professional, educational, and community boards including the Real Estate Board of New York, the Foreign Policy Association, the Center for New York City Affairs, the Helping Africa Foundation and the MBA of New York Scholarship Foundation, Inc, among others. Mr. Rose is also a founding board member of the EastWest Institute, the FC Harlem Lions youth soccer program, the Harlem Educational Activities Fund, the Forum for Urban Design, and the New York Institute for the Humanities.

Mr. Rose has been honored for his professional and community achievements by many organizations. He was named Entrepreneur of the Year by Ernst & Young in 2003 and has received the Mayor's Award of Honor for Arts and Culture from the City of New York, the Community Service Award from the Building Owners & Managers Association International, several Cicero Speechwriting awards, and the Business Leadership Award from the National Committee on Foreign Policy. His book, *Making a Living, Making a Life,* was named a Best Book of the Year in 2015 by the Kirkus Review of Books. Mr. Rose was also inducted as a fellow of the American Academy of Arts and Sciences alongside his wife, Joanna Semel. Additionally, in 1999, the Catalina Sky Survey discovered the main-belt asteroid 70712 and named it Danieljoanna, after Mr. Rose and wife.

In recognition of outstanding contributions to his profession and the Marquis Who's Who community, Daniel Rose has been featured on the Albert Nelson Marquis Lifetime Achievement website. Please visit *www.ltachievers.com* for more information about this honor.

ABOUT THE AUTHOR

Daniel Rose was born on October 31, 1929, attended public school in Mount Vernon, NY, then the Horace Mann School and Yale University. He spent the Korean War years as a military intelligence analyst in the U.S. Air Force.

During a 60 year career at Rose Associates, of which he is Chairman, he developed such projects as the prize-winning Pentagon City complex in Arlington, VA, the One Financial Center office tower in Boston, MA, and, as a consultant, conceived of and implemented the concept of "housing for the performing arts" for New York's Manhattan Plaza.

Winner of a number of national Cicero speechwriting awards, he has received Honorary Doctorates in Humane Letters from Long Island University; in Engineering from NYU/Polytechnic; and in Science from Technion-Israel Institute of Technology. He is a Fellow of the American Academy of Arts and Sciences. He has served as an 'Expert Advisor' to the U.S. Secretary of Housing and Urban Development and as an 'Expert/Consultant' to the Commissioner of Education, U.S. Department of Health, Education and Welfare.

A founding member of the NY Institute for the Humanities, he was also Chair of the Urban Design Forum, Chairman of the Jewish Community Centers Association of North America, Vice Chairman of the East West Institute, Vice Chairman of the Baltic American Enterprise Fund and is Treasurer of the Police Athletic League. He founded and is Chairman Emeritus of the Harlem Educational Activities Fund (www.HEAF.org).

He founded and endowed the National League of Cities/Urban Land Institute's Rose Center for Public Leadership in Land Use. As founding Chairman of the Helping Africa Foundation, he leads efforts to re-constitute and re-activate the W.E.B. DuBois Center in Accra, Ghana.

Other honors include the Ernst & Young 'Man of the Year in Real Estate', the NYC Mayor's Award of Honor for Art & Culture and the W.E.B. Du Bois Award from Harvard University.

He serves on multiple corporate and philanthropic boards, has been married for 63 years, has four children and eleven grandchildren.